Certified Ethical Hacker (CEH) Foundation Guide

Sagar Ajay Rahalkar

Apress®

Certified Ethical Hacker (CEH) Foundation Guide

Sagar Ajay Rahalkar
Pune, Maharashtra
India

ISBN-13 (pbk): 978-1-4842-2324-6   ISBN-13 (electronic): 978-1-4842-2325-3
DOI 10.1007/978-1-4842-2325-3

Library of Congress Control Number: 2016959970

Managing Director: Welmoed Spahr
Lead Editor: Nikhil Karkal
Technical Reviewer: Parag Patil
Editorial Board: Steve Anglin, Pramila Balan, Laura Berendson, Aaron Black, Louise Corrigan,
    Jonathan Gennick, Robert Hutchinson, Celestin Suresh John, Nikhil Karkal, James Markham,
    Susan McDermott, Matthew Moodie, Natalie Pao, Gwenan Spearing
Coordinating Editor: Prachi Mehta
Copy Editor: James A. Compton
Compositor: SPi Global
Indexer: SPi Global
Artist: SPi Global

Distributed to the book trade worldwide by Springer Science+Business Media New York, 233 Spring Street, 6th Floor, New York, NY 10013. Phone 1-800-SPRINGER, fax (201) 348-4505, e-mail orders-ny@springer-sbm.com, or visit www.springeronline.com. Apress Media, LLC is a California LLC and the sole member (owner) is Springer Science + Business Media Finance Inc (SSBM Finance Inc). SSBM Finance Inc is a **Delaware** corporation.

For information on translations, please e-mail rights@apress.com, or visit www.apress.com.

Apress and friends of ED books may be purchased in bulk for academic, corporate, or promotional use. eBook versions and licenses are also available for most titles. For more information, reference our Special Bulk Sales–eBook Licensing web page at www.apress.com/bulk-sales.

Any source code or other supplementary materials referenced by the author in this text are available to readers at www.apress.com. For detailed information about how to locate your book's source code, go to www.apress.com/source-code/. Readers can also access source code at SpringerLink in the Supplementary Material section for each chapter.

Printed on acid-free paper

To my (late) mom, my supportive dad, my loving wife, my caring grandmother, and all my best buddies!

Contents at a Glance

Contents

About the Author

Sagar Ajay Rahalkar is a seasoned information security professional with close to 10 years of comprehensive experience in various vertical fields of information security. His domain expertise is mainly in cyber crime investigations, digital forensics, application security, vulnerability assessment and penetration testing, compliance for mandates and regulations and IT GRC. He holds a Master's Degree in Computer Science and several industry-recognized certifications, such as Certified Cyber Crime Investigator, Certified Ethical Hacker, Certified Security Analyst, ISO 27001 Lead Auditor, IBM certified Specialist–Rational AppScan, Certified Information Security Manager (CISM), PRINCE2, and others. He has been closely associated with Indian law enforcement and defense agencies for close to four years, dealing with digital crime investigations and related training and has received several awards and appreciations from senior officials of police and defense organizations in India.

Acknowledgments

I would like to express my sincere gratitude to many people who have been extremely helpful in getting me through this book; to all those who provided extensive support, brainstormed things, provided valuable feedback and assisted in the editing, proofreading, and design.

I would like to give a special thanks to the Apress team (Nikhil Karkal, Prachi Mehta, and James Markham) for all their effort in making this book happen from day one, and to Parag Patil for providing valuable technical input on improving the content of the book. Above all, I want to thank my wife, dad, and the rest of my family and friends, who always supported and encouraged me in spite of all the time it took me away from them.

Last but not least I would like recognize all those who have been with me over the years and whose names I have failed to mention.

Introduction

There have been drastic changes in technology over the past decade or so. The technology landscape is now shifting toward mobility, the Cloud, and the Internet of Things (IoT). Directly or indirectly, this technology change also brings new security risks along. This has given rise to a high demand for Information Security professionals across the globe. According to the few surveys available, the number of qualified Information Security professionals is far less than the actual demand.

Securing assets from a variety of threats is an interesting and equally rewarding job. There several training programs and certifications that will get you started with your career in Information Security. One such popular certification is Certified Ethical Hacker from the EC-Council. This certification is quite comprehensive and intensive, covering various aspects of ethical hacking. The best thing is that it doesn't need any prequalification. Anyone with a keen interest in hacking and security can opt for this certification. Because the course syllabus is vast, however, it can take a lot of effort to grasp all the concepts. This book is essentially a foundation guide that covers not only the basics of hacking but also other basic prerequisites that will help you understand the core topics in a better way. Going through this book before you take the CEH course and certification will ease the process of absorbing knowledge during the course. An appendix describing various Information Security career paths and another on interview preparation have also been included to guide the reader after successful completion of CEH certification. I wish all readers the very best for their career endeavors and hope you find this book to be valuable.

PART I

CHAPTER 1

■ ■ ■

Operating System Basics

The operating system is at the core of any computing system. It acts as a foundation for other applications and utilities. The goal of this chapter is to introduce some basic concepts of operating systems from an ethical hacking perspective.

■ **Key Topics** Windows: Windows authentication, the Windows Registry, the Windows Event Viewer, Windows security and audit policies, file system basics, processes, Windows Firewall. Linux: What is a kernel?, file system structure, important Linux commands, Linux security basics.

What Is an Operating System?

Computers don't directly understand human languages. All they understand is binary machine language (0s and 1s). But for humans, it's extremely difficult to communicate with computers in that form. Software programs are the interfaces between humans and computers that help both to communicate with each other easily. There are two categories of software: *system software* and *application software*. An operating system is the system software that helps manage and coordinate all hardware and software resources. Common tasks include device management, multitasking, user management, memory allocation, and so on. The operating system also provides a base or foundation for the execution of other application software. Some of the most widely used operating systems are Microsoft Windows, Linux (Red Hat, Fedora, CentOS, Ubuntu, AIX, BSD, and others), and Android/iOS for smart phones and tablet PCs. The operating system plays a crucial role from the security perspective. However secure the application may be, if the underlying operating system is vulnerable and unpatched, then it becomes a soft and easy target for hackers and intruders. Hence, from a defensive as well as an offensive perspective, it is important to familiarize yourself with the basics of an operating system and get acquainted with various security features that the operating system offers. The following sections briefly discuss some of these features.

What Is a Kernel?

In simple words, the kernel is the core of the operating system. It has full control over all the activities that occur in the system, and it is the first program that is loaded on startup. A few of the important tasks performed by the kernel are *memory management, device management,* and *managing system calls.* The kernel does the critical job of connecting and interfacing application software with the hardware devices.

© Sagar Ajay Rahalkar 2016
S.A. Rahalkar, *Certified Ethical Hacker (CEH) Foundation Guide*, DOI 10.1007/978-1-4842-2325-3_1

The Ring Architecture

For fine-grained security, operating systems implement a concept called *protection rings*, as shown in Figure 1-1. The ring levels are classified based on their respective access privileges. The kernel, which is the core of the operating system, is at Ring 0 and has the highest privilege, meaning it has full and complete control of all computing resources (hardware and software).

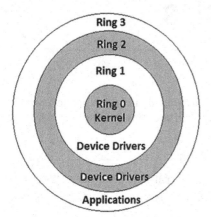

| Ring 0 | Highest Privilege |
| Ring 3 | Least Privilege |

Figure 1-1. *The ring architecture of an operating system*

The higher the ring level, usually the lower are the privileges. The application software that is installed as an add-on has the least system access privileges because it can't be trusted easily. The operating system tries to protect the ring boundaries; however, from a security perspective, nothing can be more dangerous or harmful than an attacker executing a malicious code/program with kernel-level privileges (at Ring 0).

What Is a File System?

A file system defines how data will be stored or retrieved from the storage devices. There are various file systems available; they differ in various factors like the size of data to be allowed for storage, their directory structure, naming conventions, method of buffering, and so on. Some of the common file systems in use are listed in Table 1-1.

Table 1-1. *Types of File Systems Used By Various Operating Systems*

Operating System	File Systems Used
Microsoft Windows	FAT16, FAT32, NTFS
Linux and its derivatives	EXT2, EXT3, EXT4, XFS, ReiserFS, YAFFS
MAC OS	HFS+

What Are Device Drivers?

While the file system helps in storage and management of data, an operating system also needs an interface for interacting with various types of devices that are attached to the system, such as audio/video devices, gaming devices and so on. Device drivers are a special type of software program used for interfacing between the hardware device and the operating system. Whenever we plug in a new hardware device, the operating system detects it and starts looking for a suitable device driver. Most contemporary operating systems have a set of common device drivers for various hardware devices. There are some hardware devices whose device driver is not present in the operating system by default; in such case the device driver can be installed from the media (CD/DVD) supplied with the device. Some malicious programs even try to modify device drivers to get unauthorized control over the system.

Memory Management: Stack versus Heap

Whenever we execute an application, a lot of work is carried out in the background. When the application is executed, the operating system has to allocate a memory region to store the application's temporary data. This is part of the operating system's memory management. Two common ways of allocating memory to an application are stack-based and heap-based memory allocation.

- **Stack-Based Memory Allocation**: The stack is a special-purpose area of the computer memory that is used to store temporary variables created by various function calls in the application being executed. The stack operates in a last-in, first-out (LIFO) manner. Whenever a new variable is declared, it is pushed onto the stack. When the function exits, all the variables on the stack are popped or freed from the stack, and that area is made available for other functions. Hence the stack is a limited memory area that grows or shrinks as the function pushes or pops the variables. The stack memory is allocated and freed automatically.

- **Heap-Based Memory Allocation**: Unlike the stack, the heap is a memory region that is not managed automatically. The size of the heap is larger than that of the stack. Heap memory is allocated using functions such as `malloc()` or `calloc()`, and it is freed manually using functions like `free()`.

If a program is not written securely, then an attacker can craft special requests to the application that might cause the stack/heap to overflow. This results in unauthorized access of data; that is, an application may be able to view private data from the stack region of some other application.

Microsoft Windows

Now that we have seen some generic operating system concepts, let's focus on vendor-specific systems. This section introduces some important concepts related to Microsoft Windows operating systems.

Windows Authentication: Local versus Centralized

Authentication is a process by which the operating system is able to verify and allow legitimate users and restrict unauthorized ones. The most common method used for authentication is the username/password pair. (Some advanced systems allow biometric authentication as well, including fingerprint, retina scan, and so on.) It's important to understand the various techniques Windows uses to authenticate a user.

Local Authentication

In this method, Windows stores the user credentials locally on the same system. Hence the user can log in even if he or she is not connected to any network. Most of the systems used for individual or home use are authenticated locally. Windows makes use of Security Account Manager (SAM) for storing user credentials locally on the system. The path where the SAM resides is `<$Drive>:\windows\system32\config\SAM`.

The SAM stores the passwords in hashed format. There are tools that can dump the entire SAM database and then, using various techniques, an attacker can crack the hashes to get the passwords.

Centralized Authentication

For individual and home users, local authentication works fine. But in a corporate network with hundreds of systems, it is more efficient to use centralized authentication. This gives better administrative control over the user accounts and helps enforce policies easily. Beginning in Windows 2000, Microsoft introduced Active Directory (AD), which is a central database that stores a lot of information about user accounts. Active Directory provides not only centralized authentication but also authorization. And the most useful part of AD is *groups*. The AD admin can create groups of users based on various criteria (logical, physical, and so on) and then apply customized policies to selected groups. This facilitates fine-grained control over the user accounts.

The Windows Registry

The Windows Registry is a hierarchical database that contains critical low-level information about system hardware, applications and settings, and the user account profiles. Whenever you install or uninstall an application, the Registry is modified. When you make any changes in system settings, they are reflected in the Registry. For any Windows system, the Registry is extremely important, and if it becomes corrupted, then the entire Windows system might fail and stall. Most of the malware programs that can infect your system (like viruses, spyware, Trojans, and so on) also make changes to the Registry.

To access the Windows Registry, press the Windows key + R, type `regedit.exe`, and press Enter.

■ **Note** Before you make any changes to the Registry, it is important to back up its current state in case if anything goes wrong and you need to restore it to its original state.

Figure 1-2 shows what a Registry looks like in the Registry Editor.

Figure 1-2. *Windows Registry Editor*

Backing Up and Restoring the Windows Registry

To back up the existing, current state of the Windows Registry, open the Registry and choose File ➤ Export. Then save the file in a safe location.

To restore a previously saved state of the Windows Registry, open the Registry and choose File ➤ Import. Then select the backup file that you want to restore.

The Windows Event Viewer

Whenever a fraud or a system compromise happens, the incident response team will first request the system audit logs. If the compromised system has maintained sufficient audit logs of all the events, then it becomes easy to trace back the incident. If event logs are not configured and maintained, then the investigation of an incident becomes extremely difficult. The Windows operating system categorizes and stores event logs and has an application called Event Viewer to check the logs.

1. If a hacker or an attacker compromises a system, before leaving the system they will try to clear all the event logs in order to cover their tracks. Event logs can be viewed through the Windows Event Viewer application (Figure 1-3). It can be accessed by choosing Control Panel ➤ System and Security ➤ Administrative Tools ➤ Event Viewer.

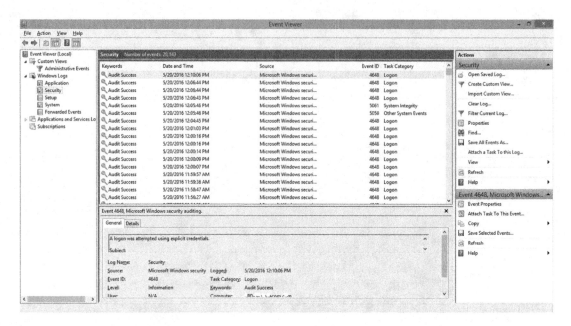

Figure 1-3. *Windows Event Viewer*

2. In Windows 7 and above you can also directly search for Event Viewer in Windows Search.

The Event Viewer has many options to search and filter the required events and acts as a comprehensive resource for auditing information.

Windows Services

A Windows service is just like any other application that you install; however, the difference is how the service functions. A service runs and performs its tasks in the background. For example, the anti-virus service starts automatically when Windows starts. When you insert a USB drive, for example, the anti-virus service, which is running in the background, automatically initiates a virus scan on the USB drive.

Some services are the result of applications that are installed explicitly, while other services run by default in a Windows system. When a system is infected, malware may be running some service in the background. So for a system administrator, it is important to monitor all the services running and disable any unwanted ones.

To manage Windows Services (Figure 1-4), press the Windows key + R, type `services.msc`, and press Enter.

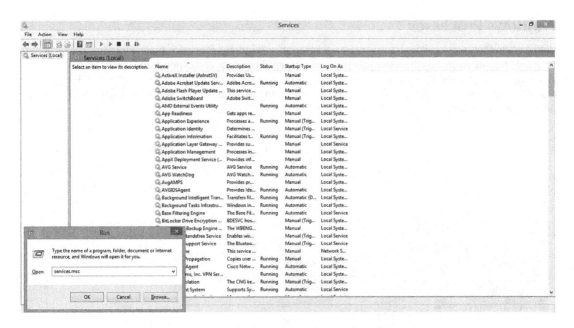

Figure 1-4. *Windows Service Manager for managing all Windows services*

If you double-click a service, you can see further details, as shown in Figure 1-5, including which application is responsible for that service, the path of the executable, and the mode of service startup (manual or automatic).

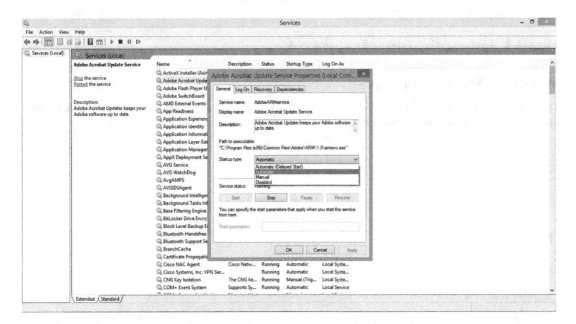

Figure 1-5. *Use this screen to start or stop any listed Windows service*

Windows Processes

Unlike a Windows service, which runs in the background, a Windows process is typically an instance of a program or application. So whenever you launch a new application, a corresponding process is spawned in the memory, and when you quit or exit the application the process is killed. To analyze in detail which processes are currently running and how they are interacting with the outside world, you can use a program called Process Explorer (available at www.sysinternals.com). See Figure 1-6.

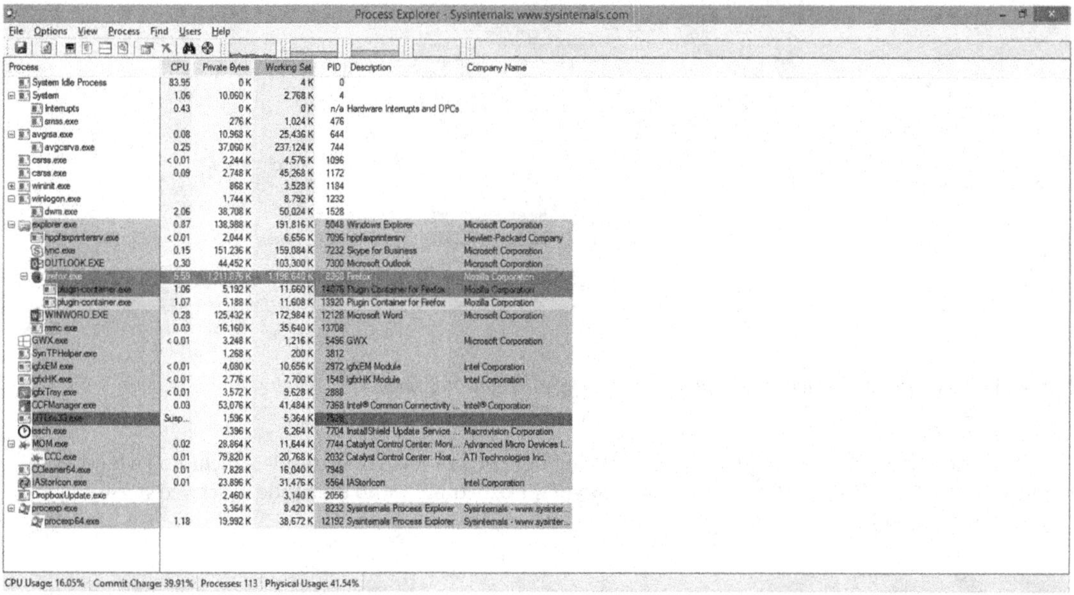

Figure 1-6. *Windows Process Explorer from sysinternals*

Windows Security Policies

The Windows operating system comes with a built-in tool known as Group Policy Editor (Figure 1-7), which helps the user or administrator configure various settings, parameters, and security policies.

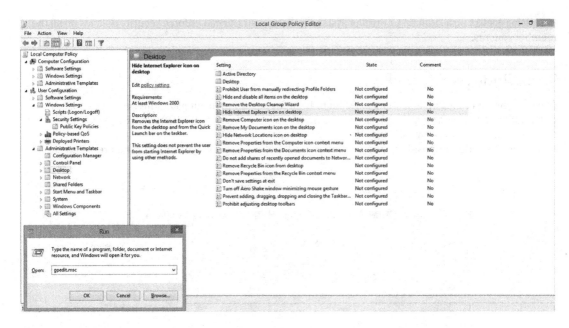

Figure 1-7. *Windows Group Policy Editor*

To get started with the tool, press the Windows key + R, type gpedit.msc, and press Enter.

You can simply double-click an item in the right pane to view more details and configure it accordingly, as shown in Figure 1-8.

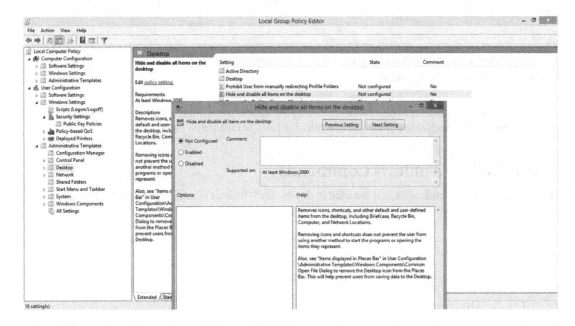

Figure 1-8. *Windows group policy editor*

Using gpedit on a Domain Controller system, an administrator can enforce security policies on all the member systems.

The Windows Firewall

The Windows operating system offers a decent built-in firewall for managing and filtering inbound and outbound traffic. It has a simple and easy to use Graphical User Interface (GUI), which helps you review existing rules and create new rules based on your needs.

To open Windows Firewall (Figure 1-9), press the Windows Key + R, type wf.msc, and press Enter.

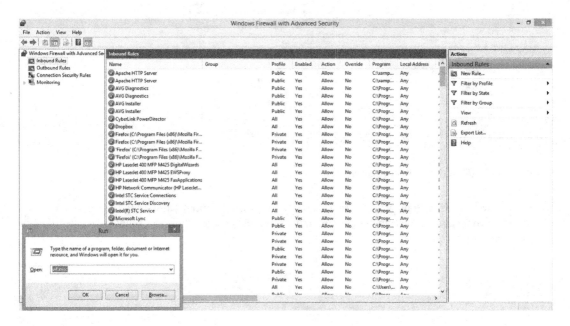

Figure 1-9. *Windows default firewall*

In the left pane, you can see the rule categories, in the middle pane you can see the existing rules for the selected category, and in the right pane you can filter the rules or create new rules.

Cheat-Sheet to Windows Commands

There are hundreds of commands that are used in day-to-day Windows administration. Table 1-2 shows some commands that are useful from a security perspective.

Table 1-2. *Some Useful Commands to Be Run from the Windows Command Prompt*

Command	Usage	Description
`tasklist`	`tasklist`	Lists all the tasks that are currently active on the system (similar to what's displayed in Task Manager).
`tracert`	`tracert <host name>`	Traces the routing path from your system to the target host.
`ipconfig`	`ipconfig /all`	Lists all network interfaces along with IP and MAC if assigned.
`driverquery`	`driverquery`	Lists all the device drivers currently installed on the system.
`cipher`	`cipher /w:<folder path>`	Makes folder content unrecoverable by overwriting the deleted data.
`assoc`	`assoc`	Lists the associations between file extensions and their corresponding programs.

Now that we have seen some essential basics about the Windows operating system, let's look at the Linux operating system in the next section.

Linux

Unlike Windows, which is a closed-source or proprietary operating system from Microsoft, Linux is open source; that is, its source code is available and one can modify it according to specific requirements. There are many versions (also called *flavors*) of Linux; some are completely free, while others provide enterprise-grade support and charge fees. Some of the most popular Linux distributions are Ubuntu, Red Hat, Fedora, and CentOS.

Linux Directory Structure

Microsoft Windows has a typical hierarchy of Drive\Directory\File. But in Linux, everything is considered a file. The root, denoted by the / symbol, is located at the top of the hierarchy.

Table 1-3 lists some of the common directories found in the Linux system.

Table 1-3. *Common Directories in Linux-Based Systems*

Directory	Description
/	The root directory of the entire hierarchy.
/bin	Stores binaries for various Linux commands like ls, cp, and others.
/boot	Contains the boot loader files.
/dev	
/etc	Stores all configuration files.
/home	Home directories for all users.
/lib	Stores library files for binaries in /bin.
/media	Mount point for external media like USB drives, CD-ROMs, and so on.
/mnt	Place for temporarily mounted file systems.
/root	Home directory for root user.
/tmp	Place for storing temporary files.
/var	Place for storing files whose content change frequently, such as log files.

Passwords in Linux

Two important files in the Linux system are responsible for storing user credentials:

- /etc/passwd is a text file that stores all the account information (except the password) required for user login. The following sample entry from an /etc/passwd file will help clarify its components:

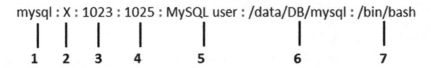

1. User Name: This is the username used to log in.

2. Password: The X character implies that encrypted password for this user is stored in the /etc/shadow file.

3. User ID (UID): Each user on the system has a unique ID. UID 0 (zero) is reserved for the root user.

4. Group ID (GID): This is the group ID of the group to which the user belongs.

5. User ID Info: This comment field can store additional information about the user, including email, telephone number, and so on.

6. Home Directory: This is the default directory that will be available for the user after login. All the user-specific documents and settings are stored in the respective home directory.

7. Command/Shell Path: This is the path to the command prompt, or *shell*.

- /etc/shadow is a text file that stores actual passwords in hashed format. It also stores parameters related to the password policy that has been applied for the user. Following is an example entry from the /etc/shadow file:

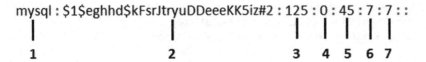

mysql : 1eghhd$kFsrJtryuDDeeeKK5iz#2 : 125 : 0 : 45 : 7 : 7 : :

1   2   3   4   5   6   7

1. Username: This is the username to which the password belongs.

2. Password: This is the password stored in hashed format.

3. Last password change: This field indicates the number of days since the last password change.

4. Minimum Age: This denotes the number of days remaining before the user can change his or her password.

5. Maximum Age: This denotes the maximum number of days after which the user must change his or her password.

6. Expiry Warning: This denotes the number of days before which the user must be warned about the password expiring.

7. Inactive: This is the duration in days after password expiry that the account will be disabled.

Linux Permissions in a Nutshell

In Linux there are three types of permission groups or classes:

- User: The owner of the file belongs to this category.

- Group: All the members of the file's group belong to this category.

- Other: All users who are neither part of the user category nor the group belong to this category.

Following are the permission types that can be applied to a file in Linux:

- Read: Gives the user access/permission to read the file. It is denoted by r and has the value 4.

- Write: Gives the user access/permission to write to the file. It is denoted by w and has the value 2.

- Execute: Gives the user access/permission to execute the file. It is denoted by x and has the value 1.

To view the permissions for a particular file, open the terminal and type ls -l <filename>. You'll see a display like the following:

```
root@ubuntu:/home/sagar/Desktop# ls -l server-stats.php
-rwx------ 1 sagar sagar 111 Mar 10  2016 server-stats.php
```

If you wish to change the permissions for a file, you can use the command chmod. As an example, to grant all file permissions to all users and groups we can use the following command:

```
chmod 777 <filename>
root@ubuntu:/home/sagar/Desktop# chmod 777 server-stats.php
root@ubuntu:/home/sagar/Desktop# ls -l server-stats.php
-rwxrwxrwx 1 sagar sagar 111 Mar 10  2016 server-stats.php
```

In this example, the chmod command is used to change the file permissions. Since we wanted to allow all permissions (read (4), write (2) and execute (1)) to the owner, the group, and others, we passed a parameter of 777. To assign only read and write permissions to the owner, the parameter value would be 600 (Read (4)+Write (2)).

Processes

A process is simply a running instance of a program. Some processes start by default on boot, while others are started when the user explicitly invokes a new program. In Linux, the ps command is used to list processes that are currently running.

To list all processes currently running, open up a terminal and type ps -A.

This command lists all the current processes along with the process ID (PID):

```
root@ubuntu:~# ps -A
  PID TTY          TIME CMD
    1 ?        00:00:01 init
    2 ?        00:00:00 kthreadd
    3 ?        00:00:00 ksoftirqd/0
    4 ?        00:00:00 kworker/0:0
    5 ?        00:00:00 kworker/0:0H
    6 ?        00:00:00 kworker/u256:0
    7 ?        00:00:01 rcu_sched
    8 ?        00:00:00 rcuos/0
    9 ?        00:00:00 rcuos/1
   10 ?        00:00:00 rcuos/2
   11 ?        00:00:00 rcuos/3
   12 ?        00:00:00 rcuos/4
   13 ?        00:00:00 rcuos/5
   14 ?        00:00:00 rcuos/6
   15 ?        00:00:00 rcuos/7
   16 ?        00:00:00 rcuos/8
   17 ?        00:00:00 rcuos/9
   18 ?        00:00:00 rcuos/10
```

To find out if a particular process is running, we can use the grep command to filter the output. For example, to see whether Firefox is running, we can run the command ps -A | grep firefox and see the following result:

```
root@ubuntu:~# ps -A | grep firefox
 3644 ?        00:00:05 firefox
root@ubuntu:~#
```

Understanding the Linux Firewall (IP tables)

The default firewall in Linux systems is named `iptables`. Covering `iptables` in depth is beyond the scope of this chapter; however, we can look quickly at the basics.

IP tables have three sections, which are referred to as *chains*:

- Input Chain: This chain is for all the packets that are destined for the local system or the packets that are inbound to the system.

- Forward Chain: This chain is for all packets that have been routed through the system and are not destined for local delivery.

- Output Chain: This chain is for all the packets that are destined for a remote system and are outbound.

Common flags or switches in `iptables` rules are shown in Table 1-4.

Table 1-4. *Common iptables Flags/Switches*

Flag	Meaning
-A	Appends a new rule to the chain.
-L	Lists the current rules for all the chains.
-p	Identifies the protocol used for the connection, such as TCP or UDP.
--dport	Matches the rule against a destination port.
-j	Performs a specified action if the rule is matched. Common actions are ACCEPT, REJECT, DROP, and LOG.
-F	Flushes, or clears, the current rule set to start afresh.

Following is a sample `iptables` rule for allowing FTP traffic:

```
iptables -A INPUT -p TCP --dport 21 -j ACCEPT
```

Let's break down this rule for a better understanding:

- Iptables -A INPUT appends a new rule to the INPUT chain of `iptables`.

- -p TCP tells the firewall to check whether the connection has been established using the TCP protocol.

- --dport 21 indicates that the rule is checking for destination port 21 (FTP).

- -j ACCEPT instructs the system to accept the packet (establish the connection) if all the previous conditions in the rule match.

In brief, this rule explicitly allows or permits all incoming requests for FTP:

```
root@ubuntu:~# iptables -A -p TCP --dport 21 -j ACCEPT
root@ubuntu:~# iptables -L
Chain INPUT (policy ACCEPT)
target     prot opt source               destination
        TCP    21           ANY
Chain FORWARD (policy ACCEPT)
target     prot opt source               destination
```

```
Chain OUTPUT (policy ACCEPT)
target     prot opt source              destination
root@ubuntu:~#
```

TCP Wrappers

The Linux system also offers a facility to allow or restrict access to various services, using *TCP wrappers*. TCP wrappers are quite simple to understand and implement. There are two files for configuring TCP wrappers:

- /etc/hosts.allow: This file contains service and client details identifying who will be allowed access.

- /etc/hosts.deny: This file contains service and client details identifying whose access is to be restricted.

First, the system checks to see if there are any records in the /etc/hosts.allow file. If there are any records, it gives access to clients according to the rules defined. If no records are found in /etc/hosts.allow, the system then checks /etc/hosts.deny and restricts or blocks access to the clients according to the rules defined. If there are also no records in /etc/hosts.deny, then as a default action, the system gives access to the client without any restrictions. Example:

```
sshd : 10.0.1.52
```

This line in the /etc/hosts.deny file says that ssh access should not be allowed from IP address 10.0.1.52.

Cheat-Sheet to Linux Commands

Beyond the common Linux commands (cd, ls, man, mkdir, rm, cp date, time, cat, echo, vi, and so on), Table 1-5 lists some of the commands that might be useful from a security perspective.

Table 1-5. *Some Common and Useful Linux Commands*

Command	Usage	Description
uname	uname -a	Returns the Linux kernel version and architecture details.
sudo	sudo <command>	Gives root privileges temporarily for running a command.
last	last	Gives details about when a particular user was last logged in.
diff	diff <folder1> <folder2>	Finds and prints differences in files present in two folders.
history	history	Prints a list of the commands that were previously fired from the terminal.
uptime	uptime	Returns the time duration for which the system has been running since the last boot, or start.
w	w	Prints details about users who have logged in with CPU usage.
crontab	crontab -l	For the current user, this command lists any scheduled jobs/tasks.
lsof	lsof	Lists files opened by the current user.
kill	kill -9 <PID>	Kills the process with the process ID passed in the argument.

Summary

Following are the key points that summarize important concepts we have learned throughout this chapter:

- An *operating system* is system software that helps manage and coordinate hardware and software resources.

- The *kernel* is the core of the operating system and has complete control over all the resources.

- Operating systems implement *ring architecture* to segregate access privilege levels for programs. Ring 0 has the highest privileges.

- The *file system* defines how files are stored into and retrieved from storage devices.

- Operating systems authenticate users using either *local authentication* or *centralized authentication* (like Active Directory or LDAP).

- The *Windows Registry* is a hierarchical database that contains critical low level information about system hardware, applications, and settings, along with the user account profiles.

- A *process* is a running instance of a program.

- / (the *root*) is at the top of the directory hierarchy in a Linux system.

- Linux allows us configure permissions for *users* and *groups*. The types of permissions available are *read*, *write*, and *execute*.

- *TCP wrappers* are used to allow or restrict access to various Linux services based on modifications in the /etc/hosts.allow and /etc/hosts.deny files.

Do-It-Yourself (DIY) Exercises

1. Dump all the password hashes from your Windows system.

2. Hide drive C: from My Computer by modifying the Windows Registry.

3. List all Login Failure events from your system using the Event Viewer.

4. Start an Internet Explorer or Firefox instance. Using Process Explorer, try to find the IP addresses of all remote systems that your browser is interacting with.

5. Set a complex password policy using gpedit.

6. Open Windows Firewall and set a rule to block all incoming SSH traffic.

7. Configure TCP Wrappers to block FTP access.

8. Write an iptables rule to block all incoming Telnet traffic.

9. Start a new browser on your Linux system. List all processes currently running on your system and, from the terminal, kill the browser process.

10. Create a new file in your Linux system and change its permissions using chmod.

Test Your Knowledge: Sample Questions

1. A process is nothing but a running instance of a program. True or False?

    a. True

    b. False

2. Which of the following Linux commands is used to check files opened by current user?

    a. `crontab`

    b. `ls -l`

    c. `lsof`

    d. `dir`

3. Which of the following files in Linux is used to store account passwords?

    a. `/etc/passwd`

    b. `/etc/passwords`

    c. `/etc/login`

    d. `/etc/shadow`

4. Which of the following commands is used to view and edit Windows Security Policies?

    a. `regedit.exe`

    b. `gpedit.msc`

    c. `wf.exe`

    d. `cmd`

5. An application running at Ring 2 has higher privileges than an application running at Ring 0. True or False?

    a. True

    b. False

6. Which of the following Linux commands is used to clear all the current `iptables` rules?

    a. `iptables -L`

    b. `iptables -F`

    c. `iptables - A`

    d. None of the above.

7. Which of the following value denotes full access (read/write/execute) to all users and groups?

    a.   555

    b.   666

    c.   777

    d.   077

8. Which of the following directories in Linux stores all configuration files?

    a.   `/var`

    b.   `/bin`

    c.   `/etc`

    d.   `/lib`

CHAPTER 2

Database Basics

The goal of this chapter is to make you familiar with basic database concepts and prepare a foundation for understanding advanced web and database attacks.

Most applications that are running today have databases at their back ends. This enables applications to store and process massive amounts of data with ease. The application just acts as a front end, but all the important data lies in the database. Hence, databases are favorite targets of attackers. If we want to defend against various database threats, we must first understand the basics about how a database operates and the languages used to communicate with it.

■ Key Topics   What is SQL? Key concepts— tables, records, fields, primary key, foreign key, procedures, important db operations, symbols in SQL.

What Is a Database?

According to the literal dictionary meaning, the word *database* is a noun that means "a structured and formal way." Now you might say that even an Excel spreadsheet can store data in a structured way, so why go for a specialized database? Well, the amount of data Excel can store is limited, as is the efficiency involved in accessing and processing the stored data. Thus, for commercial and large-scale applications, it is necessary to have database solutions integrated with the application. A relational database is a set of tables, records, and columns with a well-defined relationship between the database tables.

Widely Used Database Software

Just as we have a choice of using various operating systems like Microsoft Windows, Red Hat Linux, AIX, and so on, there are database applications available from different vendors. While some are free and open source, the others are mainly for commercial use. Some of the widely used database applications are

- MySQL
- PostgreSQL
- Oracle
- SQLite
- MS SQL Server

© Sagar Ajay Rahalkar 2016
S.A. Rahalkar, *Certified Ethical Hacker (CEH) Foundation Guide*, DOI 10.1007/978-1-4842-2325-3_2

ACID Properties

Atomicity, Consistency, Isolation and Durability (ACID) are the set of properties that ensure the reliability of database transactions. A database transaction is defined as a sequence of actions/operations that are performed as single logical unit of work.

- **Atomicity**: Atomicity means that each transaction must be "all or nothing": if one part of the transaction fails for some reason, then the entire transaction must also fail, and the database state is left intact. This helps to maintain the correct database state in case of situations like power failures, errors, and crashes.

- **Consistency**: The consistency property ensures that any transaction will transform the database from one valid state to another.

- **Isolation**: The isolation property ensures that the concurrent/simultaneous execution of multiple transactions will result in a system state that would be the same had the transactions been executed serially; that is, one after the other.

- **Durability**: The durability property ensures that once a transaction has been committed successfully, it will remain so, even in the case of power failure, crashes, or errors.

What Is SQL?

Most of us are familiar with programming languages like C, C++, Java, C#, PHP, and so on. These programming languages help us interact with the computer and develop applications. Similarly, for database systems, SQL (Structured Query Language) is used to interact and communicate with a relational database. It is a simple-to-understand language that empowers you to perform various operations on a database.

Important Database Concepts

A database has several components and entities. The following section introduces several key database terms that you need to know.

Tables: A table within a relational database is a set of values structured using vertical columns and horizontal rows. The intersection of a row and column is called a *cell*.

Records: In the context of a relational database, a record is a *row*, also known as a *tuple*.

Columns: In the context of a relational database, a column is a set of data values belonging to a particular type.

Example: **Table Name: country**

Country_id	Country	Last_update
1	India	03/05/2014
2	France	04/05/2014

In this table, (1, India, 03/05/2014) is one record or tuple and Country, with the data values India and France, is a column.

Primary Key: A primary key is a special relational database table column that uniquely identifies all table records. It always contains a unique value for each row of data and it cannot contain null values.

Example: **Table Name – country**

Country_id	Country	Last_update
1	India	03/05/2014
2	France	04/05/2014

In the above table, country_id: is a primary key and each value must be unique. It cannot recur or be duplicated anywhere in the table.

Foreign Key: In the context of relational databases, a foreign key is a field in one table that uniquely identifies a row of another table using the primary key of the linked table. This is mainly used to establish a link between two tables.

Example: **Table Name – country**

Country_id	Country	Last_update
1	India	03/05/2014
2	France	04/05/2014

In the country table, country_id is the primary key. In the city table, country_id is the foreign key. This is used to establish a link between the city and country tables.

Example: **Table Name - city**

City_id	City	Country_id	Last_update
1	Delhi	1	
2	Beijing	4	

Data Definition Language: CREATE, ALTER, RENAME, DROP, TRUNCATE

The Data definition language within SQL contains a set of commands to define structures in a database. It allows you to create new tables, rename existing tables, or remove tables from an existing database.

CREATE

CREATE is used to create a new table within the existing database:

```
CREATE TABLE table_name
(
column_name1 data_type(size),
column_name2 data_type(size),
column_name3 data_type(size),
....
);
```

Example:

```
CREATE TABLE `country` (              //Row 1
`country_id` int(5) NOT NULL,         //Row 2
  `country` varchar(10) NOT NULL,     //Row 3
`last_update` date NOT NULL           //Row 4
)
```

Row 1 instructs the database engine to create a new table named country.

Row 2 says to create a column named country_id within the table country. The value in it must be an integer no greater than 5, and it cannot be null.

Row 3 says to create a column named country within the table country. The value in it must be alphanumeric with a length no greater than 10, and it cannot be null.

Row 4 says to create a column named last_update within the table country. The value in it should be of type Date, and it cannot be null.

ALTER

ALTER is used to modify the structure of an existing table. Consider the following table:

country_id	country	last_update
1	India	2016-05-03
2	France	2016-05-03
3	Australia	2016-05-03
4	China	2016-05-03
5	Brazil	2016-05-03
6	India	2016-05-03
7	Australia	2016-05-03

Let's alter it:

```
ALTER TABLE country ADD capital int;
```

Here is the modified table:

country_id	country	last_update	capital
1	India	2016-05-03	NULL
2	France	2016-05-03	NULL
3	Australia	2016-05-03	NULL
4	China	2016-05-03	NULL
5	Brazil	2016-05-03	NULL
6	India	2016-05-03	NULL
7	Australia	2016-05-03	NULL

DROP

DROP is used for dropping or removing a table or entire database. For example, to remove a table from the current database, the following syntax is used:

```
DROP TABLE table_name;
```

TRUNCATE

TRUNCATE is used to delete all the data in a table:

```
TRUNCATE table table_name;
```

Data Control Language: GRANT, REVOKE

The data control language within SQL is used to control access to the data stored in a database. It can be used to allow or restrict various operations on a database to a particular user.

GRANT

GRANT is used to grant access rights or privileges to a particular user:

```
GRANT create table to sysuser;
```

This command would grant the privilege of creating a table to the user named sysuser.

REVOKE

REVOKE is used to revoke the privileges that were granted earlier to a user:

```
REVOKE create table from sysuser;
```

This command would revoke the privilege of creating a table from the user named sysuser.

Query and Clauses: SELECT, FROM, WHERE, GROUP BY, HAVING, ORDER BY, DISTINCT

To understand the clauses that can be used in a SQL query, let's consider the following table sample data:

Table Name: country

Country_id	Country	Last_update
1	India	2016-05-03
2	France	2016-05-03
3	Australia	2016-05-03
4	China	2016-05-03
5	Brazil	2016-05-03
6	India	2016-05-03
7	Australia	2016-05-03

SELECT and FROM

SELECT is one of the most common operations in SQL. SELECT is used for retrieving data from one or more tables. Because the SELECT statement is only for reading the data, it has no persistent effect on the database. The FROM clause is required in every SELECT statement to choose the table from which the data has to be retrieved.

```
SELECT * FROM `country`
```

Here is the output:

country_id	country	last_update
1	India	2016-05-03
2	France	2016-05-03
3	Australia	2016-05-03
4	China	2016-05-03
5	Brazil	2016-05-03
6	India	2016-05-03
7	Australia	2016-05-03

WHERE

The WHERE clause is used in conjunction with the SELECT clause to retrieve only specific records matching the criteria:

```
SELECT * FROM `country` WHERE country_id=1
```

Here is the output:

country_id	country	last_update
1	India	2016-05-03

The query returned only one record corresponding to country_id = 1. (Since country_id is the primary key, no duplicate record can be found in same table.)

GROUP BY

The GROUP BY clause is used for aggregating values in a given table.

```
SELECT * FROM `country`
GROUP BY country
```

Here is the output:

country_id	country	last_update
3	Australia	2016-05-03
5	Brazil	2016-05-03
4	China	2016-05-03
2	France	2016-05-03
1	India	2016-05-03

HAVING

The HAVING clause is used to filter data based on the group or aggregate functions. It is similar to the WHERE condition but is used with group functions. (Group functions are default SQL functions that operate on groups of rows and return a single value/result for the entire group.) Group functions cannot be used in a WHERE clause but can be used in a HAVING clause.

```
SELECT column1, column2
FROM table1, table2
WHERE [ conditions ]
GROUP BY column1, column2
HAVING [ conditions ]
ORDER BY column1, column2
```

ORDER BY

The ORDER BY clause is used to alter the order in which items are returned. We can retrieve the table data sorted in ascending or descending order.

```
SELECT * FROM `country`
ORDER BY country_id DESC
```

The table will be retrieved in descending order of country_id:

country_id ▼ 1	country	last_update
7	Australia	2016-05-03
6	India	2016-05-03
5	Brazil	2016-05-03
4	China	2016-05-03
3	Australia	2016-05-03
2	France	2016-05-03
1	India	2016-05-03

DISTINCT

The DISTINCT clause is effective for removing the duplicates in the table data.

```
SELECT DISTINCT country FROM country
```

This will remove the duplicate country names and return the distinct values.

country
India
France
Australia
China
Brazil

Data Manipulation: INSERT, UPDATE, DELETE

Data manipulation commands in SQL are used to add, modify, or remove data from existing tables in the database.

INSERT

The INSERT INTO statement is used to insert new records in the existing table:

```
INSERT INTO table_name VALUES (value1,value2,value3,...);
```

31

Example:

```
INSERT INTO Country  (country_id,country,last_update)
          Values ('1','India','2016-05-03')
```

UPDATE

The UPDATE query is used to modify existing records in any of the existing tables:

```
UPDATE table_name SET field1=new-value1, field2=new-value2
```

Example:

```
UPDATE Country
          SET last_update='2016-06-05'
          WHERE country_id='1'
```

DELETE

The DELETE query is used to delete existing records in any of the existing tables:

```
DELETE FROM table_name
WHERE [condition];
```

Example:

```
DELETE FROM Country
        WHERE country_id='1'
```

The Significance of Symbols in SQL

Every SQL query includes some symbols that are used for various purposes. It is essential to know the relevance of these symbols in order to understand the construction of SQL queries.

Symbol I	Name	Description
;	Semicolon	The semicolon character in SQL is used as a statement terminator.
--	Hyphen Hyphen	Anything that is written after this is commented out.
'	Single Quote	Single quotes are used as delimiters in a query.

Query Processing Internals

Throughout this chapter we have seen many different queries and clauses, but it is equally important to understand how a query is processed internally to give us the required output. These internals will help you understand the behind-the-scenes actions involved in query processing and more easily detect attacks based on SQL queries. Following are the high-level steps involved when we fire a SELECT query:

1. The database parser engine scans the SELECT statement and logically breaks it into smaller units such as keywords, expressions, operators, and identifiers.

2. A *query tree*, also known as a *sequence tree*, is built. It lists the logical steps involved in transforming the source data into the format required by the result set. A *result set* is a set of rows containing data as requested in the query.

3. The query optimizer selects the series of steps that returns the results fastest while using minimal resources. The query tree is updated to record this exact series of steps. The final and optimized version of the query tree is called the *query execution plan*.

4. The relational engine starts executing the query execution plan and requests the storage engine to pass the data requested up from the row sets in the relational engine.

5. The relational engine processes the data returned from the storage engine and returns the result set to the client.

Remember, the input coming from the variables of a SQL query must be treated as data only. If someone passes code through a query variable, it shouldn't be executed. This prevents potential attacks like SQL injection, which we will study in later chapters.

Summary

The following key points summarize important concepts that we have learned throughout this chapter:

- A *relational database* is a structured set of data held in a computer, especially one that is accessible in various ways.

- Some of the commonly used database applications are MySQL, PostgreSQL, Oracle, and MS SQL, among others.

- *Atomicity, Consistency, Isolation, and Durability (ACID)* are the set of properties that ensure the reliability of database transactions.

- *SQL (Structured Query Language)* is used to interact and communicate with a database.

- A *primary key* is a special relational database table column that uniquely identifies all table records.

- A *foreign key* is a field in one table that uniquely identifies a row in another table.

- DROP is used to drop/remove a table or entire database, and TRUNCATE is used to delete only data, while keeping the table structure intact.

- GRANT is used to assign privileges to a database user, and REVOKE is used to revoke the granted privileges.

Do-It-Yourself (DIY) Exercises

1. Download XAMPP [for Windows] or LAMPP [for Linux]. Install it and open up phpMyAdmin. Try to create a new sample database with the sample table and execute queries that we learned in this chapter.

2. Change the password for the root user of MySQL.

Sample Questions

1. You can add a row using SQL in a database with which of the following?

   a. ADD

   b. CREATE

   c. INSERT

   d. MAKE

2. The command to remove a table customer from a database is:

   a. REMOVE TABLE CUSTOMER;

   b. DROP TABLE CUSTOMER;

   c. DELETE TABLE CUSTOMER;

   d. UPDATE TABLE CUSTOMER;

3. Which one of the following sorts rows in SQL?

   a. SORT BY

   b. ALIGN BY

   c. GROUP BY

   d. ORDER BY

4. DROP and TRUNCATE both are used for same purpose. True or false?

   a. True

   b. False

5. Which of the following is not an ACID property?

   a. Consistency

   b. Isolation

   c. Durability

   d. Availability

6. A SQL query is terminated by which of the following symbols?

    a. Single quote

    b. Double quote

    c. Exclamation mark

    d. Semicolon

7. In SQL, which of the following commands is used to select only one copy of each set of duplicate rows?

    a. `SELECT UNIQUE`

    b. `SELECT DISTINCT`

    c. `SELECT DIFFERENT`

    d. None of the above

8. Which of the following is an aggregate function in SQL?

    a. `CREATE`

    b. `GRANT`

    c. `GROUP BY`

    d. All of the above

9. Which of the following are possible vulnerabilities in a database?

    a. Using `DELETE` to delete table data

    b. Using the `DROP` command

    c. SQL injection

    d. All of the above

10. The `FROM` SQL clause is used to do what?

    a. Specify which table we are selecting or deleting data `FROM`

    b. Specify the range for a search condition

    c. Specify a search condition

    d. None of the above

■ ■ ■

CHAPTER 3

Networking Basics

The goal of this chapter is to make you familiar with key concepts and terminology related to computer networking and network security.

In the early computer era, systems were isolated and not connected with each other. The introduction of computer networks, however, completely changed the computing perspective. Today, network connectivity has become absolutely essential. But when a system is connected to a network, it becomes exposed to many different threats and carries a high risk of being compromised. Hence, to understand various network related risk scenarios, it is essential to understand the basics of networking.

■ **Key Topics**   OSI & TCP/IP models, IP address structure and sockets, private IP vs public IP, IP V6 basics, DNS concepts, DHCP, ARP, NAT, ACLs, VPN, introduction to various networking devices.

The Open System Interconnection (OSI) Model

When we speak about computer networking, the most basic model that helps us understand how data travels across the network is Open System Interconnection (OSI). This is a conceptual model that helps us visualize and understand how communication between two or more systems occurs. The OSI model breaks the communication system into seven abstract layers as shown in Table 3-1.

Table 3-1. *The Seven Layers of the OSI Model*

Layer	Examples
Application Layer	Telnet, SSH, FTP, SMTP, HTTP, NFS, SNMP
Presentation Layer	JPG, PNG, GIF, MPEG, ASCII, CSS, HTML
Session Layer	RPC, SCP, TLS
Transport Layer	TCP, UDP
Network Layer	IP V4, IP V6, ICMP, IPsec
Data Link Layer	MAC, PPP, ATM, HDLC, Frame Relay
Physical Layer	Ethernet, ISDN, USB, DSL

© Sagar Ajay Rahalkar 2016
S.A. Rahalkar, *Certified Ethical Hacker (CEH) Foundation Guide*, DOI 10.1007/978-1-4842-2325-3_3

Here is a description of each layer:

1. **Physical Layer**: Layer 1, the physical layer, is responsible for transmitting and receiving raw bit streams and packets over a physical medium like DSL, Ethernet, USB, and so on.

2. **Data Link Layer**: Layer 2, the data link layer, provides peer-to-peer data transfer and acts as a link between two connected peers. It also offers services like flow control and frame synchronization.

3. **Network Layer**: Layer 3, the network layer, facilitates the switching and routing of data packets.

4. **Transport Layer**: Layer 4, the transport layer, ensures correct and transparent data transfer between end systems and is also responsible for recovery and flow control.

5. **Session Layer**: Layer 5, the session layer, helps initiation, management, and termination of connections between applications. The session layer sets up, coordinates, and terminates conversations, exchanges, and dialogues between the applications at each end. It deals with session and connection coordination.

6. **Presentation Layer**: Layer 6, the presentation layer, does the job of formatting the data to be presented to the application layer. It can be viewed as the translator for the network. This layer can translate data from a format used by the application layer into a common format at the sending end, and then translate the common format to a format known to the application layer at the receiving end. Data compression and encryption occurs at this layer.

7. **Application Layer**: Layer 7, the application layer, is the OSI layer closest to the end user, which means that both the OSI application layer and the end user interface directly with the application software.

The TCP/IP Model

The TCP/IP model was developed by the US Department of Defense's Project Research Agency (ARPA, later DARPA) as a part of a research project of network interconnection to connect remote computers. The objective behind the idea was to allow one application on one computer to talk (send data packets) to another application running on a different computer.

Table 3-2. *The Four Layers of the TCP/IP Model*

Layer	Examples
Application Layer	HTTP, Telnet, SMTP, FTP, TFTP, SNMP, DNS
Transport Layer	UDP, TCP
Internet Layer	IP, ICMP, ARP
Network Access Layer	Ethernet, Frame Relay

1. **Application Layer**: The application layer defines how host programs interface with transport layer services to use the network.

2. **Transport Layer:** The transport layer provides communication session management between host computers. It defines the level of service and status of the connection used when transporting data.

3. **Internet Layer**: The Internet layer packages data into IP datagrams, which contain source and destination address information that is used to forward the datagrams between hosts and across networks. It performs routing of IP datagrams.

4. **Network Access Layer**: The network access layer specifies in detail how data is physically sent through the network, including how bits are electrically transmitted by hardware devices that interface directly with a network medium, such as coaxial cable, optical fiber, or twisted-pair copper wire.

Comparing the OSI and TCP/IP Models

Now that we have seen both the OSI and TCP/IP models individually, let's compare how the two models are related to each other. The OSI Model has seven layers, while the TCP/IP model has four layers. However, layers from both these models can be logically related to each other. Table 3-3 shows the logical head-to-head comparison between the two models.

Table 3-3. *The OSI and TCP/IP Models Compared Head to Head*

Layers in TCP/IP Model	Equivalent Layers in OSI Model
Application Layer	Application Layer, Presentation Layer, Session Layer
Transport Layer	Transport Layer
Internet Layer	Network Layer
Network Access Layer	Data Link Layer, Physical Layer

TCP Vs UDP

Transmission Control Protocol (TCP) and User Datagram Protocol (UDP) are the most commonly used transport layer protocols. There are numerous applications and services that are completely dependent on one or the other of these two protocols. Table 3-4 shows a comparison.

Table 3-4. *Differences between TCP and UDP*

TCP: Transmission Control Protocol	UDP: User Datagram Protocol
TCP is a connection-oriented protocol; that is, a valid connection between systems is established before data is transmitted.	UDP is a connectionless protocol. No prior connection is established before initiating data transfer.
Applications that require high reliability for data transfer make use of TCP.	Applications for which reliability of data transfer isn't the most important consideration make use of UDP.
TCP takes more time to transmit data compared to UDP.	UDP is faster than TCP since it doesn't consume time in establishing a connection or in error correction.
FTP, HTTP, HTTPS, Telnet, and SMTP are a few of the protocols that use TCP.	DNS, DHCP, TFTP, SNMP are a few of the protocols that use UDP.
The header size in TCP is 20 bytes.	The header size in UDP is 8 Bytes.
TCP offers error detection and recovery and hence ensures that all data reaches its destination intact.	Since UDP is connectionless and doesn't offer error recovery, there's no guarantee that all data will reach the destination intact.

TCP Handshake and TCP Flags

A TCP packet has six flags that are set to either ON or OFF during communication. These flags are used for various purposes, such as initiating a session, acknowledgement, prioritization, and finishing the session. It is important to understand these flags since many of the attacks and related techniques depend on manipulation of these flags.

1. **URG**: This flag is used to inform a receiving host that certain data within a segment is urgent and should be prioritized.

2. **ACK**: This flag is set to indicate acknowledgement of received data.

3. **PSH**: This flag informs the receiving host that the data (in buffer) should be pushed up to the receiving application immediately.

4. **RST**: This flag is used to abort a connection as a response to an error.

5. **SYN**: This flag is set and used for initiating a new connection.

6. **FIN**: This flag is used for closing a connection.

Figure 3-1 shows the communication between two peers while establishing a TCP connection.

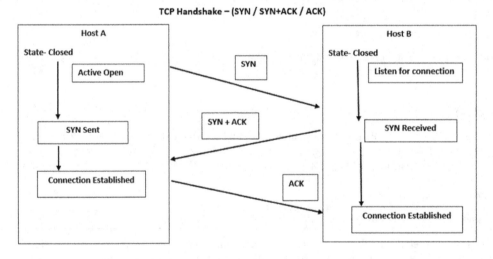

Figure 3-1. *TCP three-way handshake*

Since TCP is a connection-oriented protocol, the two communicating systems need to establish a connection by performing a handshake before actual data transfer is initiated. It is known as a *three-way handshake* and involves the following steps:

1. Host A sends a TCP **SYN**chronize packet to Host B. (This means the SYN flag in TCP packet is set ON).

2. Host B receives the SYN request sent by Host A.

3. Host B replies with **SYN**chronize **ACK**nowledgement (this means the SYN and ACK flags in TCP packet are set ON).

4. Host A receives the SYN-ACK sent by Host B.

5. Host A sends final **ACK**nowledgement to Host B.

6. Host B receives ACK sent by Host A.

7. The TCP connection between Host A and Host B is established.

For ending/terminating a connection, a similar three-way handshake is performed with the FIN flag set. The handshake follows the sequence of ➤ FIN+ACK ➤ ACK. This process is also known as *TCP teardown*.

IP Addressing and Sockets

We humans identify each other by our names and surnames. The human brain finds it easy to remember names. However, that's not the case with computers. Computers don't understand human language, nor can they communicate with each other by calling out names as humans do. So, in simple terms, an IP (Internet Protocol) address is nothing but a unique name that computers use to identify and communicate with each other. The first widely used version of IP was IP V4; let's see what an IP V4 address looks like:

XXX	.	XXX	.	XXX	.	XXX
0-255		0-255		0-255		0-255

An IP V4 address has four places separated by three decimals. Each place can have any value ranging from 0 to 255, as shown in Table 3-5.

Table 3-5. *Valid and Invalid IP V4 Addresses*

Valid IP V4 Address	Invalid IP V4 Address
192.168.1.1	192.168.301.289
10.255.201.86	154.4.89
172.51.16.78	655.453.192.1
110.45.89.201	187.245.211.101.5

Private IP and Public IP

Consider an example of a company having a main branch office and 50 employees at work. The company can't afford to get a separate telephone connection for each employee, so it gets a single telephone line and shares it among all employees using extensions. The same concept is used in the computing world. If there are multiple computers that have to be connected to the Internet, getting a separate Internet connection for each of them would not be feasible and cost-effective. Instead, a single Internet connection is taken and then shared among multiple computers.

So when you get an Internet connection, you actually get a public IP address, and this public IP address is shared among multiple computers by using private IP addresses. Thus a company pays only for a single public IP and shares it among many private IPs, which are free to use.

The Internet Assigned Numbers Authority (IANA) has provided clear guidelines on which IP addresses can be used as public and which ones as private (Table 3-6).

Table 3-6. *Private IP Address Ranges*

Private IP addresses		
Starting IP	Ending IP	Number of Hosts
10.0.0.0	10.255.255.255	16,777,216
172.16.0.0	172.31.255.255	1,048,576
192.168.0.0	192.168.255.255	65,536
Localhost IP		127.0.0.1

All the IP addresses that fall outside the ranges shown in Table 3-6 are considered to be public IP addresses . The localhost IP 127.0.0.1 is the default IP address for a local computer and is used mainly for testing purpose only.

Remember, within a network, there can never be two or more systems with the same IP address. Each system is always identified by a unique IP address.

To see your private IP address, do the following:

- In Windows, open a command prompt and enter `ipconfig /all`

- In Linux, open a terminal and type the command `ifconfig`

To check your public IP address on either operating system:

- Open `www.whatismyip.com` in your favorite browser.

Port Numbers

We have seen that an IP address is used for uniquely identifying a computer. The next important concept to understand is that of *port numbers*. Consider a computer A running multiple applications like a browser, a chat application, an email client, and so on, simultaneously. A user on computer B wants to send a chat message to the user on Computer A. By knowing the IP addresses, Computer A and Computer B can identify each other. But how does computer B ensure that chat data is sent exactly to the chat application that is running on computer A? This is achieved using port numbers. Each application on a computer that needs to communicate over a network listens on a particular port number. This ensures that correct data is sent and received by the application. Table 3-7 lists some of the commonly used port numbers.

Table 3-7. *Common Applications and Port Numbers*

Application	Port Number
FTP	20-21
Telnet	23
SMTP	25
DNS	53
TFTP	69
HTTP	80
POP3	110
NTP	123
Microsoft RPC	135
NetBIOS	137-139
LDAP	389
HTTPS	443

Port numbers 0–1024 are reserved for privileged services and are well-known ports (Figure 3-2). Ports 1025–65536 are free to be assigned and used randomly by any application. For example, 10.1.45.23:80 is referred to as a socket.

Sockets –

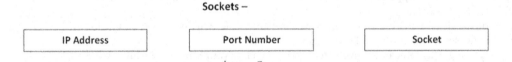

Figure 3-2. *A socket consisting of IP address and port number*

IP V6 Basics

IP V4 uses 32-bit addressing, which generates up to 4,294,967,296 addresses. As the use of technology has increased exponentially over the years, however, the IP V4 addresses are being depleted. To create more address space, IP V6 was introduced.

IP V6 uses 128bit addressing, which generates a massive address space of 655,570,793,348,866,943,898,599. Let's see what an IP V6 address looks like:

XXXX: XXXX: XXXX: XXXX: XXXX: XXXX: XXXX: XXXX

XXXX can range from 0000 to ffff, so an IP V6 address has eight places separated by seven colons:

`2002:db8:0:1:1:1:1:1`

MAC Addresses

So far we have seen that an IP address is a logical address that a computer uses to communicate with any other computer on the network. For smooth network communication, there's another type of address required, known as a *MAC (Media Access Control) address*. This is the physical address of the Ethernet card/adapter used to connect a computer in a network. Each Ethernet card has a unique MAC address, which is assigned to it by its manufacturer. The MAC address is permanent and cannot be changed under normal conditions. To check the MAC addresses of all the network adapters on your Windows system, use the following command:

```
C:\Users\Sagar>getmac /v

Connection Name Network Adapter Physical Address    Transport Name

=============== =============== ====================
WiFi            Intel(R) Wirele 80-86-F2-55-D8-B3   Media disconnected

Ethernet        Realtek PCIe FE EC-F4-BB-80-3D-82   Media disconnected
```

Introduction to DNS

So far in this chapter, we have seen that computers are uniquely identified by IP address, the same way humans are identified by name. Now, the human brain can easily remember multiple names and surnames. At any particular moment, you can tell the names of at least 15–20 people who are your friends or belong to your family. But what would happen if you are told to remember 15–20 IP addresses? That would be a tough thing, wouldn't it?

The solution to this problem is the DNS, the Domain Name System. It does a very simple job of translating IP addresses to human-friendly host names.

Whenever you type the name of a website in the address bar of your browser, the browser first asks the DNS server for the corresponding IP address of that website. Only when the DNS responds with the IP address is a further connection with the remote system established. Without the DNS, we would have to literally remember the IP addresses of all the websites that we visit on a daily basis.

To see how the translation of IP to host name works, just go to a command prompt (on Windows) or terminal (on Linux) and enter the following command:

```
nslookup google.com
C:\Users\Sagar>nslookup google.com
Server:  inf5.bnet.ssd.co.in (#This is the DNS server that responded to the query)
Address:  10.101.6.203

Non-authoritative answer:
Name:    google.com
Addresses:  2404:6800:4009:806::200e
          216.58.199.174 (#IP address for Host Name - google.com)
```

DHCP: Dynamic Host Control Protocol

We have already seen what an IP address is and looked at its structure. Any given IP address can be classified into two types: static IP and dynamic IP.

For a computer to communicate over a network, an IP address is absolutely essential. When a computer connects to a network, an IP address is assigned to it. When the same computer disconnects from and reconnects to the network, it may or may not get the same IP address as obtained previously. This depends on the type of IP address, whether it is static or dynamic.

A static IP address is one that stays persistent. That means once a static IP is associated with a computer, no matter how many times the computer may disconnect and reconnect to the network, its IP address remains same.

By contrast, a dynamic IP address is allocated to a computer only for a particular session/duration. For instance, suppose a computer connects to a network and gets an IP address. Now when it disconnects and reconnects to the network, it will get a new IP address, which is different from the previous one. So for each new network session, a new IP address is leased to the computer.

DHCP is the protocol responsible for dynamically allocating IP addresses to systems. If a computer doesn't wish to have a static IP, it communicates with the DHCP server to get a temporary IP address for that particular session.

Most computers or systems that act as servers need to have a static IP, while end-user systems more often use dynamic IP addresses.

DHCP makes use of the User Datagram Protocol (UDP) for its communication. A DHCP server runs on UDP port 67, while the DHCP client works on UDP port 68.

ARP: Address Resolution Protocol

We have already seen how DNS works, converting a host name to an IP address and vice-versa. However, in computer networking, translation/conversion between IP address and MAC is also required. This conversion is made using a protocol called Address Resolution Protocol (ARP). Speaking in terms of the OSI model, ARP converts Layer 3 (network) addresses to Layer 2 (data link layer – MAC) addresses (Figure 3-3).

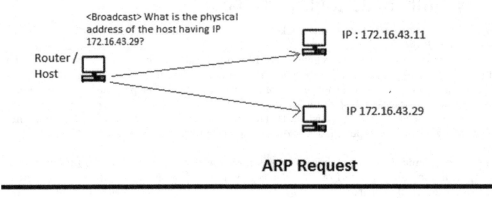

ARP Request

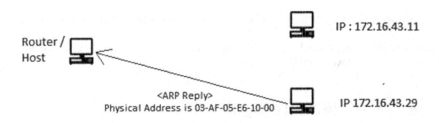

ARP Response

Figure 3-3. *Functioning of Address Resolution Protocol (ARP)*

Network Address Translation: NAT

To understand the concept of Network Address Translation (NAT), let's return to a typical telephone analogy. There's an office with one telephone line, and it is shared with multiple private connections using extensions. So when someone having an extension dials out a number, the receiver on the end sees the incoming call from the main telephone number and not from the extension. Similarly, if some external user wants to talk to a person within the organization, they must first dial the main telephone number followed by the extension. If they don't know the extension of the person they wants to talk to, they probably would need assistance from the telephone operator to get the correct extension.

The same is the case with computer networks. We have already seen that a single public IP address is shared among multiple private IPs. When someone from an external network wants to connect with one of the private IPs within the network, they must first establish a connection with the network's public IP and then hop over to the private IP. This process is simplified using Network Address Translation, shown in Figure 3-4. NAT helps by translating and forwarding connections from a public IP to a private IP. This ensures that the entire process of reaching a private IP from an external network becomes transparent and abstract to end users.

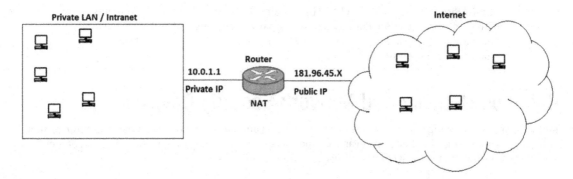

Figure 3-4. Network Address Translation for sharing a single public IP among multiple private IPs

Access Control Lists: ACL

An access control list, as the name suggests, is used to regulate and control access to resources. In the context of computer networks, ACL is mainly implemented on devices like routers, switches, and firewalls. An ACL is basically a set of rules that are applied to IP addresses and/or ports to restrict the access to only legitimate users. An access control list can be configured to regulate both inbound and outbound traffic. The Linux operating system offers network-level access control via a module called iptables. The following examples illustrate what an access control rule looks like and how it functions:

```
iptables -A INPUT -s "192.168.67.53" -j DROP
```

This rule will block all incoming traffic originating from IP 192.168.67.53.

```
iptables -A INPUT -p tcp --destination-port 21 -j DROP
```

This rule will block all incoming traffic destined for port 21 (FTP).

```
iptables -A INPUT -m mac --mac-source 00:11:2f:8f:f8:f8 -j DROP
```

This rule will block all incoming traffic originating from MAC address 00:11:2f:8f:f8:f8.

VPN (Remote Access VPN, Site-to-Site VPN)

A Virtual Private Network (VPN) is an encrypted tunnel between two hosts/systems that allows them to communicate securely over an untrusted network like the Internet. A VPN sets up an encrypted channel for secure data transfer and ensures data confidentiality, authenticity, integrity, accounting, and nonrepudiation. Remote and external users can use VPNs to access their organization's network, and depending on the VPN's implementation, they may have most of the same resources available to them as if they were physically at the office.

There are two common types of VPN:

- **Remote Access VPN**: This type of VPN is mainly used by individuals to connect to a corporate network remotely. For example, a company might have many sales executives who have to be in the field or at a client site. Such sales executives can access their company's private network securely using remote access VPN.

- **Site-to-Site VPN**: This type of VPN is used mainly for connecting two or more sites of the same organization. For example, a company might have its head office in Paris and a branch office in Sydney. To connect these two offices and to facilitate secure data transfer, a site-to-site VPN can be used.

Common Network and Network Security Devices

Just as a typical computing system is made of common input and output devices (keyboard, monitor, printer, and so on), a network is also made up of various types of devices, including routers, switches, and others. This section introduces the most commonly used networking devices.

Routers and Switches

Routers and switches are both computer networking devices that permit one or more computers to be connected to other computers, networked devices, or other networks . Table 3-8 compares the devices.

Table 3-8. *Differences between Routers and Switches*

Router	Switch
A router is used for connecting two or more networks, which may be distinct.	A switch is used for connecting two or more nodes within the same or a different network.
Data transmission is in the form of packets.	Data transmission is in the form of frames (however, Layer 3 switches transmit data in form of packets).
Routers are network layer (Layer 3) devices.	Switches mainly operate at the data link layer (Layer 2).
Routers are capable of performing Network Address Translation (NAT)	Switches cannot perform Network Address Translation (NAT)
Routers use IP address for data transmission	Switches use MAC address for data transmission

■ **Note** Frames are protocol delivery units (PDUs) operating at OSI model Layer 2 (the data link layer), while packets are PDUs operating at OSI model Layer 3 (the network layer).

Firewall, IDS, and IPS

The three devices commonly used to provide security are the firewall, the IDS, and the IPS.

Firewall

A *firewall* is a network security system that actively monitors and regulates the inbound and outbound network traffic based on a predefined security ruleset. A firewall typically acts a barrier between a trusted, secure internal network and an outside network, such as the Internet, which may not be secured enough. A firewall helps screen out malicious users, viruses, and worms that try to access your network from the Internet.

Some firewalls are simply software that runs on your computer, while other firewalls are sets of complete hardware devices and appliances. Firewalls can operate on individual hosts but are widely implemented on the network level.

Firewalls are often used to create a Demilitarized Zone (DMZ), a physical or logical subsection of a network that separates the internal private LAN from the external untrusted network like the Internet. The resources that need to be accessed externally over the Internet, such as a web server hosting a website, are kept in the DMZ. The remaining resources, like the database server and backup servers are all kept in an internal private LAN and are not directly accessible over the Internet. Because the resources in a DMZ are directly accessible to the public, they need to be hardened for security.

Firewalls also offer a feature known as *stateful inspection*, which monitors and keeps track of all the network connections and ensures that all inbound packets are the result of an outbound request. This feature was primarily designed to prevent harmful packets from entering the network and also defend against common information-gathering techniques like port scanning.

Intrusion Detection System

Unlike a typical firewall, which functions on predefined rules, an intrusion detection system is more intelligent in the way it detects various attacks. While a firewall may just check and restrict access to a particular system (based on IP address and port), the IDS would go an extra mile to check whether the traffic contains any malicious code, which might lead to an attack. Just as an anti-virus program has a signature database of known viruses, an IDS has a signature database for known and common attacks. It checks all packets traversing the network and tries to match them against its signature database. If a match is found, it raises an alert about the attack so that the network/system administrator can take appropriate steps to prevent it.

Intrusion Prevention System

An intrusion prevention system does all the jobs that an IDS does, but it also stops the attack (by dropping packets) whenever it encounters malicious traffic in network packets. This ensures an automated response to an attack and reduces manual intervention.

Summary

The following key points summarize the important concepts that we have learned throughout this chapter:

- The Open System Interconnect (OSI) model has seven layers (the physical, data link, network, transport, session, presentation, and application layers), while the TCP/IP model has four layers (the network access, Internet, transport, and application layers).

- Transmission Control Protocol (TCP) and User Datagram Protocol (UDP) are the most commonly used transport layer protocols.

- TCP is connection oriented and reliable, while UDP is connectionless and doesn't guarantee delivery of data.

- The structure of IP V4 has four places separated by three decimals, and each place can have any value from 0 through 255.

- A public IP is used for connecting to the Internet, while private IPs are used to share a single Internet connection among many computers.

- Because the IPv4 address space is depleting, IP V6 was introduced. It has eight places separated by seven colon (:) characters. Each place can have a value from 0000 through ffff (hexadecimal).

- DNS is used for converting/translating IP address to hostname and vice -versa.

- ARP is used for converting/translating IP address to MAC address.

- DHCP is used for assigning temporary IP addresses.

- NAT is used to facilitate connection between an external system and an internal system with a private IP address.

- The Access Control List (ACL) is used to control and regulate inbound and outbound network traffic based on a predefined ruleset.

- A Virtual Private Network (VPN) is used for extending a private network over an untrusted public network like the Internet. It is implemented by creating an encrypted channel between the systems, and it ensures confidentiality, integrity, authenticity, and nonrepudiation.

- A *router* is a Layer 3 device that is used to connect two or more different networks with each other.

- Conventionally, a *switch* is a Layer 2 device used to connect two or more hosts from the same or a different network.

- A *firewall* is either software or a hardware device that helps control and regulate network traffic based on predefined rules.

- An *Intrusion Detection System (IDS)* is a system that helps detect malicious network attacks by matching packets against its signature database.

- An *Intrusion Prevention System (IPS)* detects the malicious attacks like IDS; however it also prevents them by taking necessary corrective action.

- A *DMZ* is a subsection of a network, which separates an internal private LAN from the external untrusted network like Internet.

Do-It-Yourself (DIY) Exercises

1. Try to analyze the output of the following commands:

   - `ping -t <hostname/IP>`

   - `ping -n 10 <hostname/IP>`

   - `tracert <hostname/IP> [on Windows]`

   - `nslookup <hostname/IP>`

   - `nslookup -d <hostname/IP>`

   - `ipconfig /all [on Windows]`

   - `netstat`

   - `netstat -an`

   - `netstat -ar`

   - `netstat -an | grep 22 [on Linux]`

2. Download and install Wireshark (`https://www.wireshark.org/`) and listen to network traffic on an active network interface.

3. On Windows and Linux, find the HOSTS file, which contains local DNS records. Study its contents.

4. Download an application called PuTTY and try to connect to a remote host using Telnet and SSH.

5. Visit `http://whois.net` and try finding out registrant information for any of the IP or domain of your choice.

6. Become familiar with using `iptables` on a Linux system.

7. Download, install, and become familiar with SNORT, the Open Source Intrusion Detection System.

Test Your Knowledge – Sample Questions

1. Which of the following is a device that forwards packets between networks by processing the routing information included in the packet?

   a. A router

   b. A Firewall

   c. A Switch

   d. None of the above

2. Which of the following is not a layer of the TCP/IP protocol?

   a. Application Layer

   b. Session Layer

   c. Transport Layer

   d. Internetwork layer

3. TCP is a connectionless protocol. True or False?

   a. True

   b. False

4. Port number 443 is used by which of the following?

   a. FTP

   b. SMTP

   c. HTTPS

   d. DHCP

5. Which of the following protocols is used for translating IP addresses to MAC addresses?

   a. DHCP

   b. DNS

   c. ARP

   d. UDP

6. Which of the following TCP flags is used for closing a connection?

   a. ACK

   b. RST

   c. PSH

   d. FIN

7. Is 198.111.1.256 a valid IP V4 address?

   a. Yes

   b. No

8. IP V6 addresses are made up of how many bits?

   a. 64 Bits

   b. 32 Bits

   c. 96 Bits

   d. 128 Bits

9. A DHCP server is responsible for providing which of the following to its client?

   a. MAC Address

   b. IP Address

   c. Protocol

   d. All of the above

10. Which of the following helps detect malicious attacks over a network using the signature matching technique?

   a. Router

   b. Switch

   c. Intrusion Detection System

   d. All of the above

CHAPTER 4

■ ■ ■

Programming Basics for Security Enthusiasts and Hackers

Programming essentially empowers you to interact with the computer more closely and get complicated tasks done with ease. For any security enthusiast, it is certainly important to know about programming, scripting, and automation. To make you familiar with the basics of programming and scripting, this chapter provides a brief introduction to the following:

- PowerShell

- Shell scripting

- Python

PowerShell allows automation of tasks on Microsoft Windows systems, shell scripting allows automation of administrative tasks on Linux-based systems, and Python is a general-purpose programming language equipped to do multiple tasks with minimal effort. Knowing these scripting/programming languages can help in developing new customized tools or can help in doing tasks after exploiting a target system.

This chapter will get you started with some programming and automation basics.

By the end of this chapter you will be able to automate various tasks and write small scripts and programs around computer security. This chapter covers some of the fundamental tasks that any program/script might need to perform from a security perspective, including file handling, web/networking tasks, and string manipulation.

■ **Key Topics**   Python Basics, introduction to Windows PowerShell, introduction to shell scripting.

Windows PowerShell

The Linux operating system has long offered more power and flexibility to its administrators through shell scripting. However, Microsoft Windows lacked this flexibility, because of the limited capabilities of the command prompt. To overcome this limitation, Microsoft introduced PowerShell to efficiently automate tasks and manage configurations. It is built on top of the .NET Framework and provides complete access to COM and WMI.

What is its application in hacking? If you are able to compromise a target system running Windows operating system, then using PowerShell, you can do many useful tasks.

© Sagar Ajay Rahalkar 2016
S.A. Rahalkar, *Certified Ethical Hacker (CEH) Foundation Guide*, DOI 10.1007/978-1-4842-2325-3_4

The PowerShell Integrated Scripting Environment

PowerShell offers the Integrated Scripting Environment (ISE) which can be used to fire commands at runtime as well as develop and test new PowerShell scripts.

To access the PowerShell ISE, press the Windows key + R and enter `powershell_ise.exe`.. You will then see the screen shown in Figure 4-1.

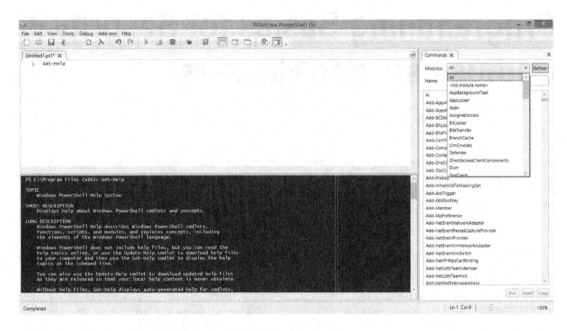

Figure 4-1. *Windows PowerShell integrated scripting environment*

In the upper-left pane, you can write new scripts, in the lower-left pane you can see the results after executing your scripts/commands, and on the right you can see all the default commands available in PowerShell.

Logic Building

Every programming language has basic constructs and logical decision-makers that are building blocks of a program. These include variables, functions, and decision-makers. The following sub-sections introduce the basic constructs in Windows PowerShell.

Variables

Variables are basic data structures to hold values. For example:

```
PS C:\Users\Sagar> $var = "Hello World"

PS C:\Users\Sagar> echo $var
Hello World

PS C:\Users\Sagar>
```

In this example we declared a new variable called $var, assigned the string value "Hello World" to it, and then printed the value the variable $var contains.

If Else Decision Making

The keywords If and Else are used for simple condition checking. If a condition is TRUE, then some action is performed; else (if it's FALSE), then some other action is performed. For example:

```
PS C:\Users\Sagar> $value = 4

PS C:\Users\Sagar> If ($value -gt 0) {"The number is bigger than Zero"} Else {"The number is
less than Zero"}
The number is bigger than Zero
PS C:\Users\Sagar> $value = -1
PS C:\Users\Sagar> If ($value -gt 0) {"The number is bigger than Zero"} Else {"The number is
less than Zero"}
The number is less than Zero
```

The above simple code checks whether the number in the variable $Value is greater than or less than zero. The script is simple and trivial to understand.

For Loops

A FOR loop is a simple control flow statement that is commonly used to perform a task repetitively using iterations:

```
PS C:\Users\Sagar> for ($i=1; $i -le 10; $i++){$j=$i*2; Write-Host $j}
2
4
6
8
10
12
14
16
18
20
```

In this example, the first line of code uses a FOR loop to print a multiplication table of 2. It iterates from values 1 to 10, and for each iteration it multiplies the value in $i by 2, stores it in the variable $j and prints the value in $j. The Write-Host cmdlet is used to print output to the user's screen. Now that we have seen how iterative tasks can be done using a FOR loop, let's see how to combine two or more tasks using pipes.

Pipes

Using pipes is an effective way of passing the output of one command as an input to another command. The pipe is denoted by the symbol | (a vertical line).

For example, the following code first executes the ls command, which lists the contents of the current working directory. Then, using the pipe (|), we pass the output as input to another command, Select-String with the parameter paros. This will display output only if a directory or file named paros is present in the current directory.

```
PS C:\Users\Sagar> ls | Select-String Paros
```

```
paros
```

File-Handling Functions

File-handling functions are those that allow creation or deletion of files or directories on the system. These functions could be effectively used to create or remove multiple files or directories based on specified criteria.

Create a New File or Directory

Cmdlet used: New-Item.
    Usage: To create a new directory, enter

```
New-Item C:\Powershell -ItemType directory
```

> This will create a new directory called Powershell in the C drive. To create a new file, enter -

```
New-Item C:\Temp.txt -ItemType file
```

> This will create a new file called Temp.txt in the C drive.

Delete a File or Directory

Cmdlet used: Remove-Item.
    Usage: –
    To delete an existing file, enter

```
Remove-Item C:\Temp.txt
```

> This will delete a file named Temp.txt in from the C drive. To Delete all contents in a directory recursively, enter

```
Remove-Item C:\Powershell\* -Recurse
```

> This will forcefully delete all files and folders within the Powershell folder located on the C drive.

Copy Files

Cmdlet used: Copy-Item.
    Usage:

```
Copy-Item C:\Temp.txt D:\
```

> This will copy the file Temp.txt from the C drive to the D drive.

Check File Properties

Cmdlet used: Get-ItemProperty
    Usage:

```
Get-ItemProperty C:\Temp.txt
```

This will display only the basic properties of the file Temp.txt. To view its advanced properties, enter

```
Get-ItemProperty C:\Temp.txt | Format-List -Property * -Force
```

This will list detailed metadata for the file Temp.txt located on drive.C

Web / Networking Functions

Virtually every computing system today is connected to a network in some form or other (wired, wireless, and so on). The following sections list some of the Web or networking related tasks that can be achieved using PowerShell functions.

Get IP Address of Current System

Cmdlet used: Get-NetIPAddress
    Usage:

```
Get-NetIPAddress
```

This will list all network interfaces on the current system along with any IP addresses assigned to the interfaces.

List all WiFi Connections in Range

Command used: netsh.exe
    Usage:

```
netsh.exe wlan show profiles
```

This will list all SSIDs that are in range.

Fetch a file from Remote URL

Command used: wget
    Usage:

```
wget http://example.com/temp.txt -OutFile D:\temp1.txt
```

This will fetch a file called Temp.txt from http://example.com and save it to the D drive.

Now that we have seen file handling and web-related cmdlets, the next section lists some other useful cmdlets for performing system tasks.

Some Useful PowerShell Cmdlets

There are hundreds of PowerShell cmdlets available, designed to do various administrative tasks. Table 4-1 lists some of the useful cmdlets.

Table 4-1. *Useful PowerShell Cmdlets*

Cmdlet	Usage	Description
Stop-Process	Stop-Process –Name Firefox	This will forcefully close the Firefox browser if it is running.
Get-Process	Get-Process | Format-Table	This will list all processes currently running on the system in tabular format.
Get-EventLog	Get-EventLog -Log "Security"	This will print all "Security" related event logs from the current system.
Export-Csv	Get-EventLog -Log "Security" | Export-Csv D:\security.csv	This will export all "Security" related events to the file security.csv on the D drive.
Get-Service	Get-Service | Format-Table	This will print a list of all services on the current system and their status, in tabular format.
Get-Help	Get-Help Format-Table	This will print detailed usage information about the Format-Table cmdlet.
Get-CimInstance	Get-CimInstance CIM_OperatingSystem	This will get details about the operating system currently installed on the system.
Get-WmiObject	Get-WmiObject -Class Win32_UserAccount -Filter "LocalAccount='True'"	This lists all the local users on the current system.

Linux Shell Scripting

A shell script is a simple file containing Linux commands and instructions that are to be executed to perform a task.

A shell script has the following features:

- It's a plain text file with a set of Linux / UNIX commands.
- It has flow control logic (like If-Else and FOR/WHILE Loops),
- It offers I/O facilities.
- It permits the use of variables for storing data.
- Unlike C/C++ code, which is compiled, shell scripts are interpreted.
- It allows for file and directory management.

Structural Basics of a Shell Script

Every programming or scripting language has its own rules, structure, and semantics (Table 4-2). Before you can code, you must know these language-specific semantics.

Table 4-2. *Components of a Shell Script*

`#!/bin/bash`	This defines which shell is to be used to run the script.
`#`	All lines starting with #are considered comments and not executed as part of code.
`chmod +x <script_name.sh>`	Makes the shell script executable.
`./<script_name.sh>`	Executes the script.
`$`	All names starting with $ are treated as variables.

Creating Your First Shell Script

Creating a shell script is quite simple; it can be created using command-line text editors like `vi` or any graphical text editor. Following are the steps to get started with creating a shell script.

1. Open a terminal on Linux.

2. Type `touch shell.sh`.

3. Type `vi shell.sh`. (`vi` is the default command line text editor; you can use any of your favorite text editors to write shell scripts).

4. Type the following code:

```
#! /bin/bash
# This is a comment on a line - Use this space for Author info
clear
echo "Hello World"
echo "This is my first shell script"
exit 0
```

5. Save the file (To save a file in vi,- press Ctrl+ Shift+q.)

6. Make the file executable by typing `chmod +x shell.sh`.

7. To run the shell script, type `./shell.sh`.

This code does the following:

Line 1: This line defines which shell is to be used.

Line 2: Content on this line is treated as a comment and not executed as part of code.

Line 3: This clears the screen.

Line 4: This prints text "Hello World" on the screen.

Line 5: This prints the text "This is my first shell script."

Line 6: This line exits the program.

Reading Input from the User

To make programs user friendly and interactive, we need to accept input from the user, process it, and give the desired output back to the user. Reading or accepting input from user in a shell script is very simple:

```
sagar@ubuntu:~$ cat read.sh
#!/bin/bash

read -p "What is your name:" name
read -p "What is your Birthdate:" bday

echo "Hello $name, welcome to the shell system. We'll soon celebrate your Birthday on:
$bday"
sagar@ubuntu:~$ ./read.sh
What is your name:John
What is your Birthdate:1-June
Hello John, welcome to the shell system. We'll soon celebrate your Birthday on: 1-June
```

Logic Building

So far we have seen how to accept input from the user. Once the input is accepted, it's essential to process the input according to the program logic. The following section introduces few constructs that help in developing logic for the program.

If Conditions

In conversation, we often say things like "If he does this, then something might happen." So basically there's a condition and if that condition holds true, then there will be result A; if that condition holds false, then there might be some other result B. Such conditional logic building is done using If-Else statements, as described below:

```
if [ condition ]
then
   Statement(s) to be executed if condition is true
else
   Statement(s) to be executed if condition is false
Fi

sagar@ubuntu:~$ cat if.sh
#!/bin/bash

a=4;
b=5;

if [ $a == $b ]
    then
        echo "Value of a is equal to b"
    else
        echo "a and b have different values"
fi
sagar@ubuntu:~$ ./if.sh
a and b have different values

sagar@ubuntu:~$ cat if.sh
#!/bin/bash
```

60

```
a=5;
b=5;

if [ $a == $b ]
    then
        echo "Value of a is equal to b"
    else
        echo "a and b have different values"
fi
sagar@ubuntu:~$ ./if.sh
Value of a is equal to b
```

FOR Loops

A FOR loop is used to perform iterative and repetitive tasks. The following line of code iterates through a directory and displays all files present in that directory.

```
sagar@ubuntu:~$ cat for.sh
#!/bin/bash

for FILE in $HOME/Desktop/*
    do
        echo $FILE
    done

sagar@ubuntu:~$ ./for.sh
/home/sagar/Desktop/apress output
/home/sagar/Desktop/burpsuite_free_v1.6.32.jar
/home/sagar/Desktop/double redirection.png
/home/sagar/Desktop/DVWA-1.9
/home/sagar/Desktop/for loop.png
/home/sagar/Desktop/if loop.png
/home/sagar/Desktop/input redirection.png
/home/sagar/Desktop/LAMPP start
/home/sagar/Desktop/numbers.txt
/home/sagar/Desktop/numbers.txt~
/home/sagar/Desktop/read user input.png
/home/sagar/Desktop/Recovered Data
/home/sagar/Desktop/server-stats.php
/home/sagar/Desktop/shell script.png
/home/sagar/Desktop/single redirection.png
/home/sagar/Desktop/vuln
/home/sagar/Desktop/vuln.c
/home/sagar/Desktop/WebGoat-5.4.war
```

Redirection

Redirection is a powerful feature of shell scripting wherein we can redirect output of a command to file, device or even another command. Imagine a command that produces some output, which is required for processing within some other command. Instead of manually copying and passing output from one command to the other, redirection can instantly pass output to any file of our choice, which can then be readily processed by some other command or program.

Single Output Redirection

The following example shows single redirection using the > operator. The output of the ls command is dumped into a file named output.txt.

```
sagar@ubuntu:~$ ls > output.txt
sagar@ubuntu:~$ cat output.txt
Desktop
Documents
download
Downloads
examples.desktop
for.sh
for.sh~
GNUstep
if.sh
if.sh~
Music
output.txt
Pictures
Public
read.sh
read.sh~
shell.sh
shell.sh~
Templates
Videos
```

Double Output Redirection (Append)

In the previous section we saw redirection with the > operator. It wrote the output to a file. However, if we fire the same command again, then the contents of the file will be overwritten. We can use the operator >> to append output to an existing file. In the following example, ls is executed in a different directory, but its output is appended to the same output.txt file that was created earlier.

```
sagar@ubuntu:~/Desktop$ ls >> /home/sagar/Desktop/output.txt
sagar@ubuntu:~/Desktop$ cat output.txt
apress output
burpsuite_free_v1.6.32.jar
double redirection.png
DVWA-1.9
sagar@ubuntu:~/Desktop$ cd DVWA-1.9/
sagar@ubuntu:~/Desktop/DVWA-1.9$ ls >> /home/sagar/Desktop/output.txt
sagar@ubuntu:~/Desktop$ cat output.txt
apress output
burpsuite_free_v1.6.32.jar
double redirection.png
DVWA-1.9
about.php
CHANGELOG.md
config
```

```
COPYING.txt
docs
dvwa
external
favicon.ico
hackable
sagar@ubuntu:~/Desktop$
```

We have now seen that output redirection can be used to write the output of a command to a file or an output device. Likewise, it's also possible to pass input to a command via input redirection, as described next.

Input Redirection

Redirection can also be used for passing input to a particular command. In the following example we use the < operator to feed a file called numbers.txt to the command sort.

```
sagar@ubuntu:~/Desktop$ cat numbers.txt
5
4
2
1
3
sagar@ubuntu:~/Desktop$ sort < numbers.txt
1
2
3
4
5
```

So far we have seen PowerShell and shell scripting, which are used for performing repetitive administrative tasks in Microsoft Windows and Linux, respectively. In the next section we'll have an overview of the general-purpose scripting language known as Python; it is easy to learn, simple yet versatile.

Python

Python is a popular and widely used high-level programming language. Python code is easily readable. Python is an interpreted language and is platform-independent, which means that if you write a Python script on a Windows system, the same script will run on Linux as well (provided there are no Windows-specific functions used). This facilitates portability of the code. Major organizations like Yahoo!, Google, Facebook, NASA, Nokia, IBM and others are using Python for various purposes.

Getting Started with Python

The Latest version of Python is 3.5.1. However, to get started, we'll use version 2.7.X, since this version supports many libraries that have not yet been completely ported to the latest version.

Most Linux systems have Python pre-installed. For a Windows system, download and install Python 2.7.11 from
https://www.python.org/downloads/release/python-2711/

Once it is installed, there are various ways of interacting with Python:

Using the Python IDLE GUI, you can directly interact with Python. In Figure 4-2, we entered **2+2** and Python returned us the result 4. Then we passed the command print "Hello World" and Python printed "Hello World" as output on the screen.

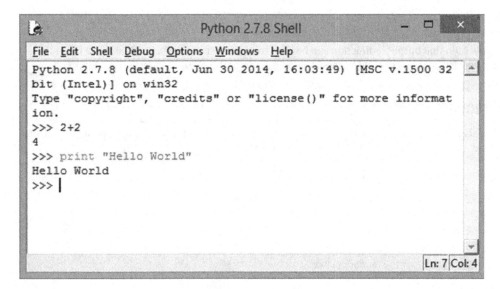

Figure 4-2. Python IDLE GUI for interactive scripting

1. In addition to direct interaction with the Python Shell, you can also use your favorite text editor to write a Python script and then execute it. Notepad++ is a very good text editor which allows for proper indentation and syntax checks. It is available at https://notepad-plus-plus.org . Save the Python program with the .py extension in order to make it executable.

Printing and Reading Input

Accepting input from the user and displaying the results back to the user are among the most common activities in any programming language. In Python it's very easy to do these tasks.

To accept input from the user we use the function raw_input(), and to display the result back to the user we use the function print().

```
name = raw_input("What is your name?")
print ("Hello '+name+', welcome to Python Class")
C:\Users\apress>read_input.py
What is your name? John
Hello John, welcome to Python Class
```

So far we have seen how to accept input from the user and store it in a variable. However, there might be a situation where it is required to store multiple elements of different data types. In such a case we need a special data type: the list, described in the next section.

Lists

For storing a single value, we typically use variables. But, there may be instances where we want to store heterogeneous elements together—that is, elements of different data types, like numbers (int), strings (char), and so on. The list is a very versatile data type in Python, because it stores elements of different data types.

For example, the program shown in Figure 4-3 creates two different lists. List1 contains string values as well as numbers, and List2 contains only numbers. Once the list has been created, any individual element in the list can be accessed by referencing its index number. The index numbering starts from zero: the first element in the list has the index value 0, the next element has the index value 1, and so on.

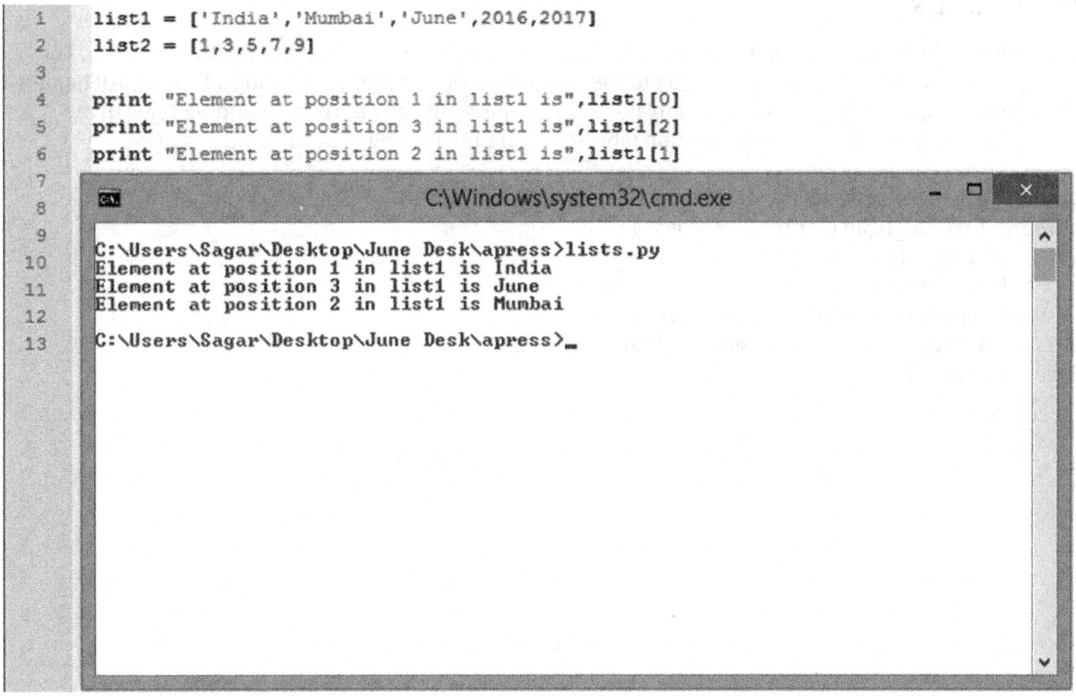

```
1    list1 = ['India','Mumbai','June',2016,2017]
2    list2 = [1,3,5,7,9]
3
4    print "Element at position 1 in list1 is",list1[0]
5    print "Element at position 3 in list1 is",list1[2]
6    print "Element at position 2 in list1 is",list1[1]
```

```
C:\Windows\system32\cmd.exe

C:\Users\Sagar\Desktop\June Desk\apress>lists.py
Element at position 1 in list1 is India
Element at position 3 in list1 is June
Element at position 2 in list1 is Mumbai

C:\Users\Sagar\Desktop\June Desk\apress>_
```

Figure 4-3. *Creating two different lists*

Conditions: IF-ELSE

IF-ELSE constructs are used for making decisions. For example, in the following code, the program accepts a number from user as an input. Then the program divides the number by two. If the remainder is zero, it displays the text "You entered an even number"; otherwise, it displays "You entered an odd number."

```
number = int(raw_input("Enter a number"))
if number % 2 == 0:
    print "You entered an even number"
else:
    print "You entered an odd number"

C:\Users\apress>"odd even.py"
Enter a number5
```

```
You entered an odd number

C:\Users\apress>"odd even.py"
Enter a number4
You entered an even number
```

In the above example we explicitly used the function int() for raw_input() because the input type is an integer number.

FOR Loops

The FOR loop in Python is a simple loop used to iterate through a range and perform tasks repeatedly. For example, the following code first accepts a number from the user as input. Then, using a FOR loop, it iterates through the range 1 to 11. For each iteration, it multiplies the number by the corresponding value in the range. Thus final output is the multiplication table for the number supplied by the user.

```
print "This is a program to display a multiplication table"
number =int(raw_input("Enter a number"))
for i in range (1,11):
    print number*i
C:\Users\apress>"multiplication table.py"
This is a program to display multiplication table
Enter a number5
5
10
15
20
25
30
35
40
45
50
```

So we now know that loops are used for performing simple tasks repetitively using iterations. However, there might be a complicated piece of code that we need to reuse in the program again and again. This can be handled using functions, as described in the next section.

Functions

Functions are used when we have to perform a particular task repeatedly within the same program. For example, in the following code, we define a new function named addition. Throughout the program, whenever we need to add two numbers, we simply call this function and pass values to it. The function then performs the required tasks and returns the result to the variable that was used to call the function.

```
def addition(number1,number2):
    result=number1+number2
    return result
```

```
print "This is a program to add two numbers"
number1 = int(raw_input("Enter first number"))
number2 = int(raw_input("Enter second number"))
output = addition(number1,number2)
print output
C:\Users\apress>"read input.py"
This is a program to add two numbers
Enter first number5
Enter second number20
25
```

File Handling

Table 4-3 lists the various functions related to file handling.

Table 4-3. *File Handling Functions*

Function	Description
Open()	Opens a new or existing file.
Close()	Closes the previously opened file and frees the system resources.
Read ('r')	Opens the file in read mode.
Write ('w')	Opens the file in write mode.
Append ('a')	Opens the file in append mode.

The following program first opens the file sample.txt in read mode and then, using a FOR loop, it displays the content of the file on the screen:

```
file_name = "sample.txt"
file = open(file_name, "r")
for line in file:
    print line
<Output from Sample.txt>
Hello World
Welcome
To
Python
Programming
```

Libraries and Modules

In any programming language, to achieve the desired output, you can either write the code yourself or you can reuse existing code written by someone else. Python is extremely rich in library functions. So if you want to do a particular task, you may not need to write all the code from scratch and reinvent the wheel! You can simply search for a suitable library, import it into your code, and call the relevant functions.

Summary

The following key points summarize the important concepts that we have learned throughout this chapter:

- PowerShell is a tool for scripting and task automation on Windows systems.
- PowerShell by default has cmdlets, which perform predefined tasks.
- A file with a PowerShell script has the extension .PS1.
- Shell scripting provides a way of automating various tasks on a Linux system.
- Pipes allow passing the output of one command as input to another command.
- Python is an interpreted scripting language.
- A file with a Python script has an extension .py.
- Python has rich support for many libraries, which can be instantly used for performing complicated tasks.

Do-It-Yourself (DIY) Exercises

1. Write a PowerShell script to automatically back up a folder on a particular day of a week.

2. Write a shell script to list current users on a system along with their last login.

3. Write a Python script to accept input from a user and write that input to a new file.

Test Your Knowledge: Sample Questions

1. Windows PowerShell is built on top of Java framework. True or False?

   a. True

   b. False

2. Which of the following is a lightweight script used to perform a single function in PowerShell?

   a. Pipe

   b. Function

   c. Cmdlet

   d. ISE

3. Is PS C:\Admin\user> ls | a valid Windows PowerShell statement?

   a. Yes

   b. No

4. Which of the following symbols is used to denote a comment in a shell script?

    a. @

    b. <!--

    c. %

    d. #

5. Which of the following commands is used to make the shell script executable?

    a. `chmod -l filename.sh`

    b. `chmod 010 filename.sh`

    c. `chmod -x filename.sh`

    d. None of the above

6. Which of the following operators is used to append text during output redirection in a shell script?

    a. >

    b. <<

    c. <

    d. >>

7. Which of the following functions in Python is used to accept input from user?

    a. `raw-input()`

    b. `read_raw()`

    c. `raw_input()`

    d. `get_inputs()`

8. Lists in Python can hold heterogeneous data types. True or False?

    a. True

    b. False

CHAPTER 5

Virtualization and Cloud Basics

As the demand for computing resources is exponentially increasing, there's high demand for new technologies that provide rapid on-demand resources to customers. This chapter introduces a few technologies designed to do that, including virtualization, containerization and cloud computing, along with their security implications.

■ **Key Topics**   What is Virtualization?, Hypervisors, Types of Clouds, Basics of Cloud Security, and Introduction to Docker.

What Is Virtualization?

Virtualization is a way of creating a virtual (rather than physical) version of something, including virtual computer hardware platforms, operating systems, storage devices, and computer network resources.
   Some of the benefits of using virtualization are:

- **Eco friendliness**: How can virtualization be eco-friendly? It's simple, in the absence of virtualization, more and more physical systems are required in the data center. To keep these systems cool, powerful air-conditioning systems are required, which contribute to global warming. With virtualization, a single server can run multiple instances of an operating system simultaneously, reducing the number of physical devices in the data center.

- **Reduced cost**: When there's a need to expand a data center, the cost of procuring new hardware can be considerable. But with virtualization solutions, the same hardware can be reused optimally to accommodate expansion needs. Hence, it clearly saves the cost involved in purchasing new hardware.

- **Faster deployment**: Suppose there's a demand for a new web server. In a physical data center, the IT team would have to set up the hardware and then the software. It would take some time for the entire process. But with virtualization, servers can be created and running within few minutes and the applications can be deployed instantly. This saves lot of time and effort.

Hypervisors

A *hypervisor* is a piece of computer software, firmware, or hardware that creates, runs, and manages virtual machines.

A system on which a hypervisor is running one or more virtual machines is called a *host machine*. Every virtual machine that runs on a hypervisor is known as a *guest machine*. The hypervisor is responsible for providing the guest operating systems with a virtual operating platform, and it manages their execution.

The Type 1 Hypervisor

A Type 1 hypervisor is also known as a *bare metal* hypervisor. It resides directly on the hardware and makes resources available for the guest operating systems (Figure 5-1).

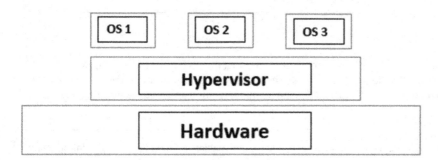

Figure 5-1. *Type I hypervisor architecture*

Type 2 Hypervisor

A Type 2 hypervisor resides on a base operating system and supports the hosting of other guest operating systems (Figure 5-2). There is a risk that if the base operating system encounters any errors, the entire virtualization stack (the guest operating systems) might crash.

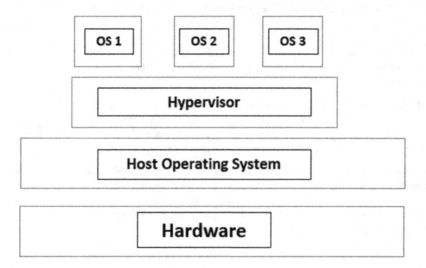

Figure 5-2. *Type 2 hypervisor architecture*

Commonly Used Hypervisors

There are many hypervisors that are widely used for virtualization; some are commercial while others are open source. Table 5-1 lists some of the commonly ones used.

Table 5-1. *Popular Hypervisors*

Hypervisor	Vendor	Type
vSphere/ESXi	VMWare	1
Hyper-V	Microsoft	1
XenServer	Citrix	1
Red Hat Enterprise Virtualization	Red Hat	1
KVM	Open Source	1
Virtual Box	Oracle	2
VMWare Workstation	VMWare	2
Virtual PC	Microsoft	2

Snapshots

Imagine you have spent two full days of effort in setting up a new operating system. Now a user wants you to install an application on it. You install the new application, but unfortunately it crashes. The new application has modified many files on your system, and you just can't figure out how to revert or roll back the changes. You might have to set up the operating system again from scratch. That can be quite painful. This is where snapshots come in handy. You can simply set up your system according to your needs and then take a snapshot. Whenever it looks like your system has undergone unwanted modifications, you can simply roll it back to the snapshot (of the last known good configuration) within a few clicks. This saves a lot of time and effort. Thus, a snapshot is nothing but a virtual machine state saved at a particular time.

Common Security Issues with Virtual Machines

In addition to the security issues in the guest system hosted in a virtual environment, the virtualization environment itself adds to certain security concerns, as described next:

- **Unpatched Hypervisor**: The hypervisor that is used to run a virtual machine is a piece of code and might be vulnerable to security issues. Often the hypervisor is not updated and patched, leaving it vulnerable to attackers. Once the hypervisor is compromised, an attacker may be able to compromise the virtual machines hosted on that vulnerable hypervisor.

- **Insecure Management Console**: Every virtualization platform has a management console or user interface through which the administrator can perform various activities, like starting or stopping the virtual machines. However this management console may be vulnerable to various security issues like XSS, privilege escalation, weak password policy, and so on. Such insecure management console would provide easy entry point to the attackers.

- **Dormant Virtual Machines**: Virtual machines can be made up and running as per the demand in very less time. However many users use a virtual machine for a few days and then simply leave it unused and unnoticed after their work is over. Such unused and dormant virtual machines could potentially be used by attackers to compromise other hosts in the network.

Creating a New Virtual Machine with Oracle VirtualBox

To demonstrate creating a new virtual machine, we'll use Oracle VirtualBox (a type 2 hypervisor) and host Ubuntu as the guest operating system. You'll first need to download and install the latest VirtualBox from www.virtualbox.org/ and download the latest Ubuntu image (ISO) from www.ubuntu.com/download/desktop.

■ **Note**   If your base operating system (the one on which Oracle VirtualBox is installed) is 32-bit, you cannot use a 64-bit guest OS.

Then open the newly installed Oracle VirtualBox and click New (Figure 5-3).

Figure 5-3.

Then follow these steps:

1. Type the name of the new VM as **Ubuntu**. VirtualBox will automatically detect its type as Linux.

2. Allocate RAM to the new VM. How much you allocate depends on how much RAM your base OS has. For example, if you have 4 GB RAM for your base OS, you can easily allocate around 1 GB RAM for the new guest VM. Steps 1 and 2 are illustrated in Figure 5-4.

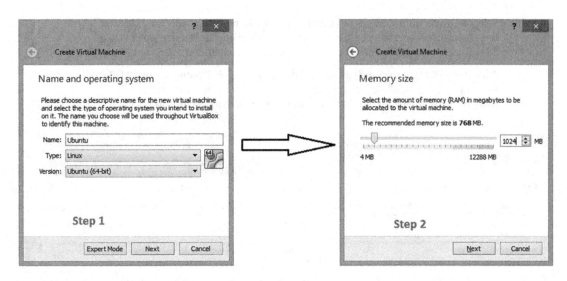

Figure 5-4. *Creating a new virtual machine using VirtualBox*

3. Create a new virtual hard drive for the new VM. If you have an existing virtual drive you can reuse it as well. Or if you just want to boot into Ubuntu using a live CD, you may even skip adding a virtual hard drive.

4. The newly created virtual drive will be stored as a file on your physical drive. You can select from various file formats available for storing the virtual hard drive. Here we select the default VDI format. Steps 3 and 4 are illustrated in Figure 5-5.

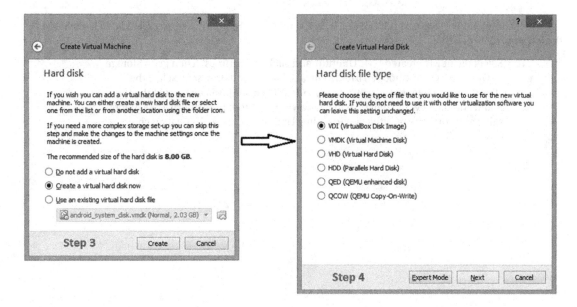

Figure 5-5. *Selecting the type of virtual hard disk for the virtual machine being newly created*

5. Select how you want to store the virtual drive file. "Dynamically allocated" means the virtual drive file size will grow only when required and "Fixed size" means that all required space will be pre-allocated irrespective of whether it's used or not.

6. Allocate the size for the new virtual hard drive. For a basic Ubuntu setup, 20 GB of space would be sufficient to start with. You can later create and attach virtual hard drives as and when required. Steps 5 and 6 are illustrated in Figure 5-6.

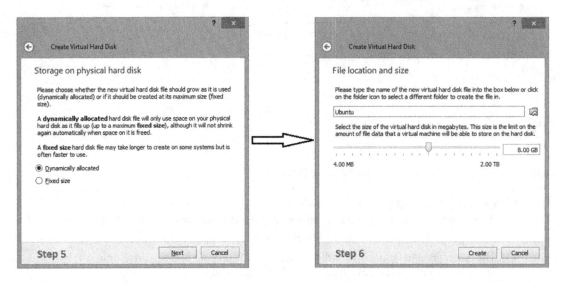

Figure 5-6. *Selecting the location where the virtual hard disk will be stored*

After completion of step 6, you'll notice a new VM named "Ubuntu" has been created and is visible in the left pane of Virtual Box.

7. Select the newly created VM "Ubuntu" and click on "Settings". Then go to Storage ➤ Optical Drive ➤ Choose Virtual Optical Disk File and browse to select the Ubuntu ISO image that you just downloaded. Then simply click Start in the top menu and the new VM will start in a new window. From here onward, it's exactly same as if you were booting and installing Ubuntu on a real physical machine (Figure 5-7).

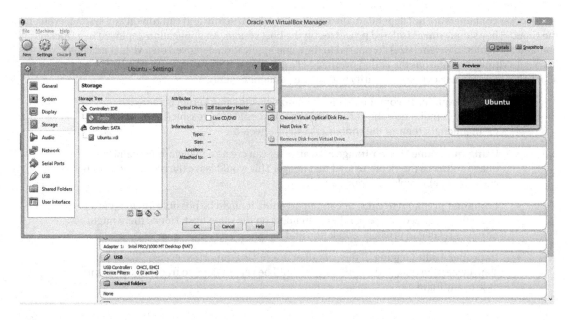

Figure 5-7. *Selecting an ISO image for booting up the newly created virtual machine*

Software Containerization with Docker

Docker is a relatively new concept that is similar to virtualization. This open source platform is a container that wraps around a piece of software such as an application and provides everything that the application needs to run (Figure 5-8). Imagine you are a system administrator and you have the task of installing and configuring the same application on 10 different servers. The application has many dependencies and complex configuration files. You might do it all on one server, but it would be painful to do such a tedious task on 10 different servers. Docker comes to the rescue in exactly this situation. With Docker, you can create a container with all application dependencies, configuration files, and everything else that the application needs to run. Once the container is ready, you can ship the container to any number of servers and run the application instantly. So Docker helps you avoid the painful task of configuring applications repeatedly on multiple systems. This is extremely cost- and time-efficient.

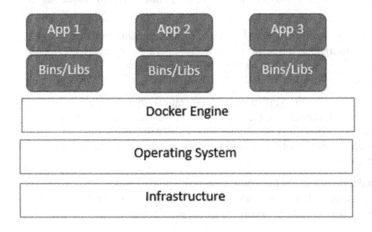

Figure 5-8. *Docker architecture*

Docker containers are not dependent on any specific infrastructure and can run on any system, even on the Cloud. They simply run as isolated processes on the host system. An application deployed in a Docker container is lighter in weight (size) compared to the same application deployed on a virtual machine, because a virtual machine has the added overhead of a guest operating system.

Following are some common security issues with containerization:

- **Kernel Exploits**: In containerization technology, the same kernel is shared across all containers. If the kernel panics or crashes for any reason (intentional or unintentional), then all the containers will be affected.

- **Using vulnerable Docker images**: An attacker can create a malicious container image and force the victim to load that image. This would leave the container as well as the host vulnerable to various attacks.

- **Container breakouts/leaks**: In containerization, it might be possible for an attacker to get unauthorized access to other containers on the same host. Hence there might be issues related to privilege escalation and leaks.

- **Improper Audit Logging**: If the container doesn't log important events (like start, stop, ownership info, and so on) then it would be very difficult to traceback events in case of any fraud.

Cloud Computing

Cloud computing, or on-demand computing, is a term used for using remote servers typically hosted on a public network like the Internet to store, process and manage data. The simple example to understand the relevance of Cloud computing is Apple iCloud. All Apple devices, including MacBook, iPhone, and iPad can be synchronized using iCloud. Let's suppose you are editing a document file on your MacBook and you need to travel without it. The document can be saved in iCloud and while you are travelling, you can use your iPhone to retrieve the partially completed document from iCloud and work on it further. This enables seamless work connectivity. Thus the Cloud technology offers on-the-fly services and features that you can use for efficient work.

Types of Cloud

Based on the purpose and type of application to be deployed, the Cloud can operate in various modes as described next:

- **Private Cloud**: Private clouds are solely owned and operated by an organization for a limited group of users. For example, a company may choose to operate a private cloud to enable its employees to do all financial, payroll and HR management activities. Access to the cloud would be limited to the employees of the company.

- **Public Cloud**: Public clouds are owned and operated by organizations that want to offer access over public network to various computing resources. For example Office 365 from Microsoft offers users access to all Office applications. Once the user signs up, he can access Office applications (Word, Excel, and so on) from any device (such as a PC, mobile, tablet and so on).

- **Hybrid Cloud**: Hybrid Cloud utilizes features from both private and public Cloud computing. A company may choose to host some features and functions in-premises for privacy reasons while getting some additional features from a publicly hosted Cloud.

Cloud Service Offerings

Cloud computing offers flexibility in terms of offerings to customers. Based on the exact requirements of the customer, following are some of the models through which Cloud services can be provided:

- **Software-as-a-Service (SaaS)**: In this type of offering, applications are hosted on servers accessible over a public network. Whenever the client demands for use of particular application, the vendor creates an application instance for the client instantly. The client can then access the application using a web browser, and all the processing is done on the server side. The client doesn't have to worry about maintenance and upgrades as it is all done by the vendor. Common SaaS offerings include email suites, customer relationship management (CRM) systems, healthcare applications, and so on. Examples: Google Apps, Citrix GoToMeeting, Cisco WebEX, and others.

- **Platform-as-a-Service (PaaS)**: This type of offering provides the customer with a platform to develop, run, and manage applications without getting involved in the complexity of developing the entire development stack from scratch. The customer has control over the custom application and its configuration, while all other components, libraries, and resources are managed by the vendor. Examples: Google App Engine, Heroku.

- **Infrastructure-as-a-Service (IaaS)**: This type of offering is best suited for startup companies that need all computing resources (network, data processing, storage) but don't want to invest in setting up their own data center. In such a scenario, the vendor provides the customer with all the resources that a data center offers. The customer can use the system on pay-per-use basis and save the cost of procuring new hardware and software. It offers better flexibility and scalability.

Benefits of Using the Cloud

There are multifold benefits to using Cloud services compared to the standard physical infrastructure. Some of the key benefits are:

- **Environment-friendly**: Because the Cloud is essentially a virtualized environment, there is much more service and resource scalability with existing hardware, resulting in less heat generation and less use of air-conditioning systems, making it more environment-friendly.

- **Better data security**: Suppose you had stored all your company confidential data on your laptop, and one day it is stolen. All the data is lost. But if the Cloud is used to store data, then your data remains in safe custody even if your laptop gets stolen.

- **Work from anywhere**: By using Cloud services, you can literally work from any remote place provided you have a basic computing device (laptop, smartphone, or tablet PC) and an Internet connection.

- **Reduced expenditure costs**: Cloud computing provides many services and resources on a pay-as-you-use basis. So if you need a server just for 15 days a month, you need not buy a physical server. You just need to subscribe to a Cloud service, which will instantly allocate you a server for 15 days and you'll be billed only for those 15 days. You can pay and use whenever you wish, as simple as that.

- **Updates and Maintenance**: If you have your own infrastructure, you have to take care of its periodic maintenance and updates. But with the Cloud, you simply concentrate on using the service or resource you subscribed for. All the maintenance and updates of the underlying infrastructure will be taken care by the Cloud service provider.   ,

- **Easy disaster recovery solutions**: For smaller organizations that can't afford to have dedicated disaster recovery sites, Cloud can offer instant DR solutions.

- **Scalability**: Today your business might need 10 servers, but after six months you might need 20 servers, and after a year you might need to scale down to only 5 servers. Meeting the fast-changing needs of the business is well served by Cloud services. The Cloud offers easy upscaling and downscaling of infrastructure.

Cloud Security Considerations

We have seen so far that the Cloud is a virtualized platform for providing on-demand services and resources to its clients. However, the software and applications that run on the Cloud are the same that would run on your physical data center. So all the vulnerabilities that apply when physical infrastructure is used apply to the Cloud as well. For example, if a particular operating system is vulnerable to denial-of-service (DoS) attacks, then it would be vulnerable on the Cloud as well as a physical machine. However, using services and resources on the Cloud has some additional security concerns which should be addressed properly before subscribing to the service.

- **Data Loss**: It might happen that the Cloud service provider has not taken enough care to back up your data. Hence your data might be at risk of not being recovered in case of accidental or intentional deletion.

- **Account Hi-Jacking**: We have already seen that many Cloud services work on a pay-as-you-use basis. Now suppose you have paid for using a particular service for 10 hours. If your Cloud credentials are leaked or compromised, the unauthorized user would simply consume and finish away your "paid" service time.

- **Insecure APIs**: Many Cloud service providers provide their customers with APIs (Application Programming Interfaces) to connect and manage cloud resources. If these APIs have security vulnerabilities then your application and the surrounding ecosystem also becomes vulnerable.

- **Denial of Service Attack**: If the Cloud service provider has not applied sufficient security controls, then the whole Cloud infrastructure may be at a risk of DoS attack. If the attackers succeed with the DoS attack, it would directly affect all the clients using that Cloud service.

- **Legal Issues**: You might be living in one country but your Cloud service provider might be in some other part of world. Thus the Cloud service provider may not be liable under the laws of the client's country. In case of any fraud or breach, the legal issues might become complex.

- **Abuse by malicious insiders**: Because the data on Cloud is virtually beyond sight and boundaries, there's a risk of data being compromised or leaked by insiders with malicious intent working within the Cloud service provider.

Summary

The following key points summarize the important concepts that we have learned throughout this chapter:

- *Virtualization* is a way of creating a virtual (rather than physical) version of something, including virtual computer hardware platforms, operating systems, storage devices, and computer network resources.

- A *hypervisor* is a piece of computer software, firmware, or hardware that creates, runs, and manages virtual machines.

- A Type 1 hypervisor is also known as a bare-metal hypervisor. It resides directly on the hardware and makes resources available for the guest operating systems.

- A Type 2 hypervisor resides on a base operating system and supports hosting of other guest operating systems.

- Some of the commonly used hypervisors are KVM, Hyper-V, and Virtual PC.

- A *snapshot* of a Virtual Machine is simply its state at given point of time.

- *Cloud computing*, or *on-demand* computing, refers to using remote servers typically hosted on public network like the Internet to store, process, and manage data.

- Public Cloud, private Cloud, and hybrid Cloud are some basic types of Cloud.

- Some of the Cloud service offerings include Software-as-a-Service, Platform-as-a-Service, and Infrastructure-as-a-Service.

- Docker is a container with all dependencies and everything else that an application needs to run.

- Docker containers are infrastructure-independent and even run on the Cloud.

Do-It-Yourself (DIY) Exercises

1. Install CentOS in a virtual machine using Oracle VirtualBox.

Test Your Knowledge – Sample Questions

1. Which of the following is not a benefit of virtualization?

   a. Virtualization technology is eco-friendly.

   b. Virtualization facilitates faster deployments.

   c. Virtualization increases overall cost.

   d. None of the above.

2. A Type 2 hypervisor resides directly on the hypervisor. True or false?

    a. True

    b. False

3. The feature of hypervisors that allows us to save the current state of a machine is called:

    a. Snapshot

    b. Freeze

    c. Backup

    d. Restore

4. Which of the following are types of Clouds?

    a. Public Cloud

    b. Hybrid Cloud

    c. Only a

    d. Both a and b

5. What is the name of the technology that wraps up piece of software or an application along with everything that the application needs to run?

    a. Cloud Computing

    b. Virtualization

    c. Docker

    d. None of the above

PART II

■ ■ ■

CHAPTER 6

Information Security Basics

This chapter introduces key concepts and terminology pertaining to information security, which will be frequently used as a base to many other concepts that are part of the CEH course.

■ **Key Topics**   The Confidentiality-Integrity-Availability (CIA) Triad, Authentication, Authorization & Accounting (AAA), Nonrepudiation, Vulnerability, Exploits, Risk, Threat, the Usability Triangle (Functionality, Usability, Security), Information Security Threats (Natural, Physical, Human), Defense in Depth, Zero Day, Daisy Chaining, Hacking Vs Ethical Hacking, Types of Hackers, Difference between Policy, Procedure, Guideline, and Standard.

Understanding the Basics: Confidentiality, Integrity and Availability

Confidentiality, integrity, and availability, often known as CIA, are the building blocks of information security (Figure 6-1). Any attack on an information system will compromise one, two, or all three of these components. Based on which of these components is being compromised the most, efficient security controls can be designed accordingly.

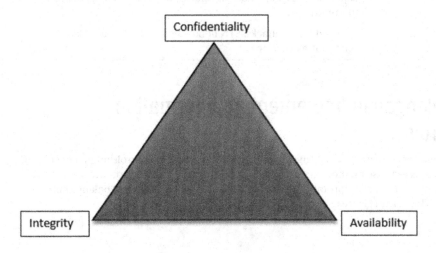

Figure 6-1. The confidentiality, integrity and availability (CIA) triad

© Sagar Ajay Rahalkar 2016
S.A. Rahalkar, *Certified Ethical Hacker (CEH) Foundation Guide*, DOI 10.1007/978-1-4842-2325-3_6

Confidentiality

In layman's terms, something that is *confidential* is secret and is not supposed to be disclosed to unintended people or entities. What's the first thing that comes to your mind that needs to be kept confidential? Probably your passwords and ATM PINs. There may be many parameters and information items that need to be kept confidential during a particular communication. If confidentiality is compromised, it might result in unauthorized access to your systems or severe loss to your privacy!

Integrity

In context of the information security (InfoSec) world, *integrity* means that when a sender sends data, the receiver must receive exactly the same data as sent by the sender. For example, if someone sends a message "Hello!", then the receiver must receive "Hello!" That is, it must BE exactly the same data as sent by the sender. Any addition or subtraction of data during transit would mean the integrity has been compromised.

Availability

Availability implies that information is available to the authorized parties whenever required. For example, consider a server that stores the payroll data of company employees. The finance team wants to access it at of fiscal year-end for some reporting purpose. If the server is able to provide all the requested information to the requestors, then its availability is considered good and healthy. But if the server goes down at all (for any intentional or unintentional reason), and the finance team is not able to retrieve required data in time, then we say that the information availability has been affected or compromised.

During an attack on a computer system, at least one of the three, confidentiality, integrity or availability, is affected or compromised. Table 6-1 shows various attacks with classification.

Table 6-1. *Various attacks on Confidentiality, Integrity and Availability*

Attacks that affect Confidentiality	Packet sniffing, password cracking, dumpster diving, wiretapping, keylogging, phishing
Attacks that affect Integrity	Salami attacks, data diddling attacks, session hijacking, man-in-the-middle attack
Attacks that affect Availability	DoS and DDoS attacks, SYN flood attacks, physical attacks on server infrastructure

Common Challenges in Implementing Information Security Controls

Quite often, end users consider security to be a form of overhead. Adding security controls might affect the functionality as well as ease-of-use for the end user. However, security is equally important in order to protect the application or system from compromise. Hence it is crucial to achieve the right balance between functionality, usability, and security (Figure 6-2).

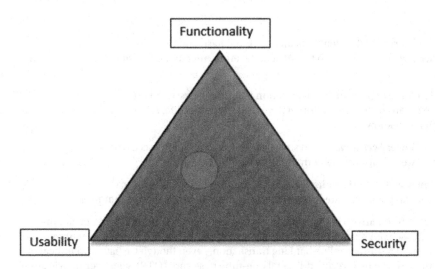

Figure 6-2. *The usability triangle*

Implementing security controls in an organization is often considered overhead. More often, the implementation of security controls becomes debatable between various stakeholders within the organization. For example, the business team (typically the business analysts and the project managers) want functionality as a priority. They would strictly want the application functionality to be developed exactly as specified during the requirements phase of the project. While end users would want all the functionality correct, they also want ease of use. The easier to use an application is, the happier end users are. And then comes the security! While most of the security controls can be made transparent to the end users, others, like two-factor authentication, can add overhead on end users. But considering the sensitivity of application data, such advanced security features may be needed. So balancing between functionality, usability, and security becomes challenging at times, since all three are equally important.

Authentication, Authorization, and Accounting (AAA)

To understand the concepts of *authentication, authorization,* and *accounting*, let's take a simple real-world example. John goes to XYZ Corporation for a job interview. He is stopped at the main entrance of the organization. The security guard asks John the purpose of his visit and his ID proof. Then the security guard calls up the relevant department to verify that they had really invited John for the interview. This is nothing but the authentication process. Once the security guard received affirmation, he made a manual entry in the visitor's book recording John's ID number and in-time. He then accompanied John to a guest meeting room. This is nothing but authorization, since John is authorized only to enter the guest meeting area and not the other departments. Now, finishing up the interview, John leaves the company premises and the security guard notes his out-time. This is nothing but accounting; that is, the security guard recorded all the important details about John's visit to the company: in time, purpose, person whom he met, out time, and ID number.

Authentication

Authentication is a process of verifying the identity of an individual based on the credentials provided. It ensures the individual is who he or she claims to be. Most of the authentication techniques rely on following three principles:

- **Something you know**: This is the most common technique. Passwords are the most common means of authentication that we use in our daily life. A Password is "something that you know."

- **Something you have**: Access cards and smart cards that enable your access to restricted areas are example of "something you have".

- **Something you are**: Biometric authentication techniques like fingerprint scan, retina/iris scan, and palm scan are some of the advanced authentication techniques.

If the system or application you are accessing contains extremely sensitive information, then at times multifactor authentication is used; for example, "something you know (the password)" plus "something you are (a fingerprint scan)". In our day-to-day online banking transactions, even though we have authenticated using our regular password, we often receive an additional one-time password (OTP) whenever we wish to make any critical transaction.

Over the last few years, there's been a new concept, called *risk-based authentication*. To understand this, let's take an example of a bank website. A person logs in into her online bank account daily from her home computer. So, from the IP address, the bank's website knows the user's usual login location. On a particular day, the person travels out of country and tries to log in to her bank account. Now the bank's website identifies that the user is logging in from a different location than usual and treats it as a risk. (There's a possibility that her account may have been compromised and someone is trying to access it from outside the country). Thus the bank's website enables multi-factor authentication in form of OTP and security questions. This approach is known as risk-based authentication.

Authorization

Once an individual is authenticated, the next action to be performed is *authorization*, which defines the access rights to be given to the individual. Authorization is typically designed through an *access control matrix*. This matrix gives a clear representation of which resources an individual is authorized to access. For example, the following sample access control matrix shows different subjects and objects, along with the relationship between the subject and the object in terms of access to resources.

Subject	Object		
	Payroll System	Finance Data System	HR Management System
John	YES	NO	YES
Tom	NO	YES	NO
Bill	YES	NO	YES

Accounting

In security, *accounting* means keeping a record of all important activities and events, typically in the form of audit logs. Events like log-in, log-out, insert/update/delete transactions, source IP, and other information are captured in audit logs. Whenever a system is breached, audit logs prove to be most vital resource in backtracking the incident and finding the root cause. If the accounting information is insufficient, investigating an incident becomes extremely difficult.

Information Security Terminology

Now that we have seen the three concepts authentication, authorization, and accounting, which govern legitimate access to a system, let's understand a few more key terms that are often misused or misinterpreted.

What Is Nonrepudiation?

Just imagine a scenario wherein you lend some money to your friend, and after few days, your friend simply denies that he ever received any money from you. You'll feel cheated, won't you? *Nonrepudiation* in simple terms means the assurance that someone cannot deny something. For example if you send a digitally signed document to your business partner, then later on you cannot deny that you sent that particular document. In the digital world, there are various ways of achieving nonrepudiation, and some will be discussed in Chapter 14, "Cryptography."

What Is a Vulnerability?

In very simple terms, a *vulnerability* is a weakness in a particular system. Let's take a real-life example. You leave your house, but you forget to shut your windows and lock your doors. Hence, your house has now become vulnerable to a thief, making a robbery possible! Another example would be if you are using a default password for your Internet account and haven't changed it since its inception. This makes your password vulnerable to various password cracking attacks.

What Is a Zero-Day Vulnerability/Exploit?

Have you ever wondered how an anti-virus application works? Basically, whenever a new virus is found, the research and development team of the anti-virus software company studies the behavior of the virus and then releases a signature to detect it along with a solution to remove the virus and clean the infected system. So most of the functioning of an anti-virus program is dependent on how updated its signature database is. But until a signature for a new virus is made, the virus is able to harm systems.

Similarly, when a new vulnerability is detected, until the time it is known to all and a patch is developed to fix it, it is known as a *zero-day vulnerability*. Such vulnerabilities are very effective for the reason that their patch has not been developed. So the affected systems are open to the risk of being exploited until a patch or some compensating control or developed. A few of the underground websites or black-hat hackers even make money selling zero-day vulnerabilities!

What Is an Exploit?

A literal meaning of the word *exploit* is utilizing something for one's own advantage. In terms of information security (InfoSec), it could be said that a vulnerability in a system can be exploited, possibly opening unauthorized access to the system. Black-hat hackers around the world continue developing exploits for various vulnerabilities. So if you know if that a system has a particular vulnerability, then you can either use any readily available exploit or develop your own exploit as well.

What Is a Risk?

The dictionary meaning of *risk* is "a situation involving exposure to danger"; from an information security perspective, a security risk is typically an event that could possibly lead to the compromising of assets within an organization. This may include gaining un-authorized access, leakage of sensitive information, tampering with data, and so on.

What Is a Threat?

A *threat* or *threat-agent* is a probable danger that might exploit an existing vulnerability in a system to gain un-uthorized access and further perform malicious activities.

Putting It All together: Vulnerability, Risk, Threat, and Exploit

To sum-up, consider a situation in which a system is connected to a network and doesn't have an anti-virus application installed on it. Now since the system is without anti-virus, it's vulnerable, which means there is a risk of a virus attack. Such a virus is a threat that exploits the vulnerability to infect the system and spread it over a network. You can see how the terms *vulnerability*, *exploit*, *risk*, and *threat* are interrelated.

Information Security Threats

It's not always a black-hat hacker or a cracker who poses a threat to information systems. There are various categories of threats that could harm assets with equal impact.

Natural Threats

Natural threats consist mainly of natural disasters like floods, storms, hurricanes, earthquakes, and so on. For instance, a company that has its data center near coast is possibly at risk of being hit by floods. Such threats can be mitigated to an extent by studying the geographical conditions of an area and then planning accordingly. Disaster recovery and contingency plans also help in such cases.

Physical Threats

Physical threats include damage caused by to theft, fire, water spillage, or collision. Fluctuating electric voltage can also impact the functioning of certain electronic devices. For example, a person might accidentally drop a hard drive, causing permanent damage to the data it contains.

Human Threats

Human threats include threats caused by human intervention, either intentionally or unintentionally. For an organization, insiders can cause as much harm as the external attackers. For example, disgruntled employees may try to steal company confidential information and sell it to the competitors.

Defense In Depth

In the previous section, we saw various types of threats. It's possible that these threats might occur one at a time or simultaneously. In such a case, additional security controls may be required in addition to the existing ones. *Defense in depth* is a conceptual approach wherein multiple layers of security controls are applied to ensure that even if control at a particular layer fails, there's adequate security on other layers to compensate and stop the attack (Figure 6-3). In the real world as well, we apply multiple layers of security to protect our valuables. In a nutshell, even if an attacker is able to bypass security at a particular layer, he would still be blocked by the security controls at the next layer, stopping him from a successful intrusion.

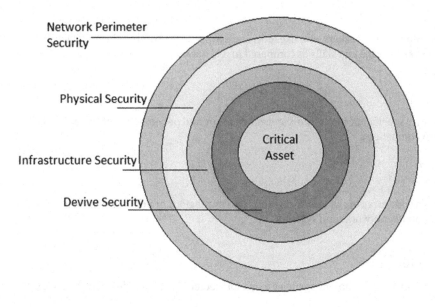

Figure 6-3. *Defense-in-depth architecture*

Types of Hackers

According to the dictionary meaning, a *hacker* is any person who usually has extraordinary computer skills and uses his knowledge to gain unauthorized access to target systems. However, in practice there are several categories of hackers, which are classified based on the intent and motive behind hacking and the method used for hacking. A few categories of hackers are discussed in the next sections.

Black Hats

These are mainly individuals with extraordinary computing skills but performing activities that are malicious or destructive in nature. They are also sometimes referred as *crackers*.

White Hats

They are individuals with relevant hacking skills who utilize their knowledge for defensive purposes (for example, to protect organizations from hacking attacks). They are also known as *security analysts*.

Gray Hats

These are individuals who work offensively as well as defensively at various times.

Suicide Hackers

These are individuals who aim to attack and bring down critical infrastructure and aren't worried at all about the consequence or the punishment they might face for their act.

Script-Kiddies

These are mainly unskilled and novice hackers who use tools and scripts developed by others to hack into systems. They don't possess knowledge and skills as compared to real hackers.

Spy Hackers

These are individuals who are specifically hired by organizations to spy and penetrate to get trade secrets and confidential data from competitors.

Cyber Terrorists

These are individuals with a wide array of skills who are motivated by religious or political agenda to launch massive attacks against computer networks and systems.

State-Sponsored Hackers

These are individuals who work for government agencies to get top-secret information from rival nations and governments.

What Is the Difference between Hacking and Ethical Hacking?

This is quite simple to understand. As an illustration, suppose a person hacks into a bank website and transfers some money to his account. This is an unauthorized transaction and is known as hacking. If caught, he might end up in jail and the bank may file a lawsuit against him. But there's another person who is hired by the bank itself to test whether its website is secure or not. So the person will try to hack into the bank's website but with prior legal and written permission from the bank. And if the person is able to hack in, he/she will inform the bank about what the exact vulnerability was and how to fix it. This is called *ethical hacking.*

As technology is advancing rapidly, the risks associated with it are also increasing at a fast pace. Thus, ethical hacking plays the important role of predicting various probable vulnerabilities and security lapses before a real attacker can exploit them. Ethical hacking also helps the organization in developing the strategy to counter threats by anticipating them in advance.

Policy, Procedure, Guidelines, and Standards

Policy, procedure, guidelines, and *standards* are terms that are often used interchangeably. But it is essential to understand the exact difference between these terms. Table 6-2 is a comparison chart that helps you understand the difference.

Table 6-2. *Comparing the Terms Policy, Procedure, Guidelines, and Standards*

Policy	Standard	Procedure	Guideline
A very high-level statement and often generic in nature.	Usually defines the acceptable level of quality.	A detailed sequence of steps to accomplish a certain task.	Simply a piece of advice, suggestion, or a best practice for how to act in a particular situation.
Usually, all the users who are governed by a policy are mandated to follow it.	May or may not be mandatory to follow.	May or may not be mandatory to follow.	Merely recommended and left to the user's discretion whether to follow.
Examples: Internet security policy, email policy, clear desk policy	Examples: ISO 27001, PCI DSS	Example: Disaster recovery standard operating procedure (SOP)	Example: Guidelines on how to set a strong password.

Incident Management

A typical computing environment is always at risk of facing various attacks from both internal and external users. Some of these attacks succeed and cause disruption of services. This raises an alarm and is termed an *incident*. Such a situation needs to be handled systematically to ensure the disrupted and affected services are restored to normal as soon as possible. Incident management is a set of processes that help identify, analyze, prioritize, and resolve security incidents and also take measures to prevent recurrence of the same incident in the future. Following are the various phases involved in incident management:

- **Detection and Analysis**: An incident is detected either manually or through some system.

- **Classification and Prioritization**: Once the incident is detected, it needs to be classified on the basis of its type and prioritized based on its severity.

- **Notification**: All the users and stakeholders that are affected by the incident need to be notified accordingly.

- **Containment**: Immediate action needs to be taken to reduce, control, or stop the damage that is being caused by the incident.

- **Investigation**: A detailed investigation needs to be made to find out the root cause of the incident and assess the damage caused by the incident.

- **Recovery and restoration**: All the affected systems need to be restored to their normal state.

- **Post-incident activities**: A detailed root cause analysis (RCA) report is prepared and discussed among stakeholders, and controls are put in place to avoid future occurrences of similar incidents.

Summary

The following key points summarize the important concepts that we have learned throughout this chapter:

- *Confidentiality, integrity,* and *availability* are the basic building blocks in information security.

- *Authentication* is the process of verifying the identity of an individual based on the credentials provided. *Authorization* is the process of assigning access rights. *Accounting* involves the process of keeping an audit trail and logs for important events and activities.

- *Nonrepudiation* is the assurance that someone cannot deny something. A *vulnerability* is a weakness in the system. An *exploit* is a way of taking advantage of a weakness in a system.

- A security *risk* is an event that could possibly lead to the compromise of assets within an organization.

- A *threat* or *threat-agent* is a probable danger that might exploit an existing vulnerability in a system to gain unauthorized access and further perform malicious activities.

- Information security threats can either be natural, physical, or human in nature.

- *Defense in depth* is a multilayered security approach wherein if one layer of security fails, another layer helps defend against the attack.

- A *zero-day* vulnerability is one that is known but for which a patch has not been developed.

- *Ethical hacking* is a process of testing the security of a system and finding vulnerabilities but with prior permission/approval from the system owner.

- *Incident management* is a methodological approach for dealing with incidents, which involves identification, classification, communication, containment, investigation, and recovery and post-incident procedures.

Do-It-Yourself Exercises

- Browse through the website `https://cve.mitre.org/` and try to find out vulnerabilities in Java, Oracle, and Microsoft Office.

- Try to explore and learn more about the Common Vulnerability Scoring System (CVSS).

- Try to find the latest zero-day vulnerabilities or at least five vulnerabilities that were zero-day in the last 6 months.

- Browse through the website `https://www.exploit-db.com/` to find exploits for various vulnerabilities.

Sample Questions: Test Your Knowledge

1. In computer security, which of the following means that computer system assets can be modified only by authorized parties?

    a. Confidentiality

    b. Integrity

    c. Availability

    d. Authenticity

2. Which of the following are mainly unskilled and novice hackers who use tools and scripts developed by others to hack into systems?

    a.   White hat hackers

    b.   Gray hat hackers

    c.   Script-kiddies

    d.   Suicide hackers

3. A procedure document contains high-level statements and is generic in nature. True or False?

    a.   True

    b.   False

4. What is a zero-day vulnerability?

    a.   A vulnerability that is known to all

    b.   A vulnerability about which no one knows at all

    c.   A vulnerability that is known but whose fix has not yet been developed

    d.   None of the above

5. Fingerprint scan is an authentication technique based on which of the following principles?

    a.   Something you have

    b.   Something you are

    c.   Something you know

    d.   None of the above

6. Denial of Service attacks affect which of the following factors?

    a.   Confidentiality

    b.   Integrity

    c.   Availability

    d.   All of the above

7. A weakness in a system is known as a:

    a.   Risk

    b.   Threat

    c.   Exploit

    d.   Vulnerability

CHAPTER 7

■ ■ ■

Penetration Testing

Penetration testing (sometimes called *pen testing*) is not just about using a handful of tools to scan the target network and generate a long report. It's a methodological process that involves many stakeholders and multiple activities. The goal of this chapter is to make you familiar with the penetration testing life-cycle, which includes various phases of the pen test, various types of security assessments, and much more.

■ **Key Topics**   Security assessments, security audits, vulnerability assessments, penetration testing, what should be tested, scope of testing, types of penetration testing, and the penetration testing lifecycle.

Why Security Assessments Are Required

Most of us are aware of quality assurance (QA) testing. It is a process that is widely accepted and followed not only in the software industry, but also in non-IT sectors like automobile manufacturing and others. The process ensures that whatever product has been developed meets certain quality criteria, and the end user or the customer will be happy and satisfied using the product. Security assessments follow quite a similar approach. When a new software application is developed or a new system is deployed, it needs to undergo security assessment in order to ensure that it is compliant with security standards and will offer the best possible protection and resilience against common threats. This also ensures that the end user gets peace of mind from using secure software. Thus, security assessments have now become an integral part of the development lifecycle.

The term *security assessment* is quite generic and has a broad meaning. More precisely, it can be classified into three categories, as shown in Figure 7-1.

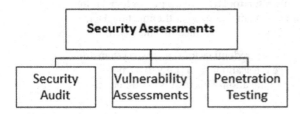

Figure 7-1. *Security assessment breakdown*

© Sagar Ajay Rahalkar 2016

S.A. Rahalkar, *Certified Ethical Hacker (CEH) Foundation Guide*, DOI 10.1007/978-1-4842-2325-3_7

Security Audits

A computer security audit is a manual technical assessment of a system or application, which focuses on people as well as processes. Every organization has a set of baselines, and the IT security audit is performed with respect to these baselines. Some of the techniques used for security audits are:

- Questioning, interacting with, and interviewing the staff and relevant stakeholders

- Performing a security review of infrastructure components like operating systems, databases, and so on

- Verifying and analyzing physical access controls for critical infrastructure

There are guidelines and checklists from various institutes like NIST, SANS, and others, which provide ready reference for performing comprehensive security audits.

A security audit systematically evaluates an organization's security posture against well-defined compliance criteria. It covers both technical and procedural functions within an organization. It helps assure the stakeholders that the organization has implemented a set of standard information security policies and has put sufficient security controls in place. Some organizations that operate in a specific domain or geographical area may need to comply with regulatory standards as well. For example, organizations operating in the health insurance domain are required to be compliant with HIPAA standards, while those handling payments are required to be compliant with PCI DSS. Thus, such organizations are required to undergo security audits based on these corresponding standards and submit a proof report for compliance at regular intervals.

Vulnerability Assessments

Vulnerability assessment or analysis is a way of defining, identifying, and classifying security issues or bugs in a computer system or network. This is typically performed using vulnerability scanners, which are capable of identifying device configurations including the type of OS they are running, ports that are open, and the applications that are installed on the target system. With the help of vulnerability scanners, one can easily identify common misconfiguration flaws, accounts with weak or default passwords, unwanted or unused services, and files or directories with weak permissions. Vulnerability scanners are also known to report false positives; that is, they may report a vulnerability that actually doesn't exist on the system being audited. Thus the vulnerability assessment report is required to undergo a manual review and verification to remove any such false positives and then present the most accurate report to the stakeholders.

The accuracy and coverage of vulnerability assessment also depends on how the scan was performed, either authenticated or unauthenticated:

- **Authenticated scan**: The vulnerability scanner is provided with valid credentials for the target system (often those of an administrator/root user). This proves to be more effective since it opens up areas of the target system that need authentication. Hence the coverage or surface area of the vulnerability scan is significantly increased.

- **Unauthenticated scan**: This is a scan where no credentials for the target system are provided to the vulnerability scanner. Hence the scanner scans only those parts of the target system that don't require any authentication. This results in limited scan coverage of the target system.

Some of the tools that are widely used for vulnerability assessments are Nessus, NExpose, and OpenVAS, among others.

Penetration Testing

Penetration testing goes beyond a vulnerability assessment to simulate the actions of a real attacker in order to gauge the impact of vulnerabilities that might be exploited. If you wish to secure and harden your infrastructure, then you must think like a real hacker and try to figure out ways of breaking into your systems and gaining unauthorized access to critical resources. However, penetration testing needs to be performed cautiously. For example, a denial-of-service (DoS attack) test run on a production server in an uncontrolled manner may result in the server crashing.

Deciding What Should Be Tested

It is important to do correct scoping for the penetration test and ensure that all important assets are tested. The pen-tester, along with the relevant stakeholders from the target organization, should review the organization's asset list and categorize and prioritize the assets based on their criticality. For instance, a public-facing website is a high-value target compared to an internal employee portal. The assets can also be prioritized based on past security incidents that they might have been subject to. Taking into consideration all such factors will result in a list not limited to the following:

- Web servers
- FTP server
- DNS
- Mail servers
- Firewalls
- IDS and IPS devices
- Remote access appliances like a VPN
- Communication links
- Public-facing websites
- Internal systems storing sensitive data (such as payroll systems)

Penetration tests may be external or internal, black-box, gray-box, or white-box, and announced or unannounced. The following sections discuss these different types of penetration tests.

External and Internal Testing

External penetration testing is the most common and conventional method used. It involves initiating tests from some remote external network so that all the test traffic passes through the target's firewall, IDS, IPS, and any other security devices deployed on the network perimeter (Figure 7-2). This scenario is similar to that of a real attacker/hacker trying to attack or gain access to the organization's resources remotely from the Internet.

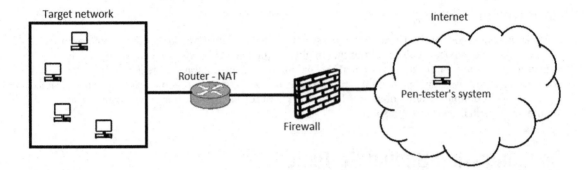

Figure 7-2. *External penetration testing with the attacker attacking from a system located in a public network like the Internet*

Internal penetration testing is performed from within the network of the target organization (Figure 7-3).

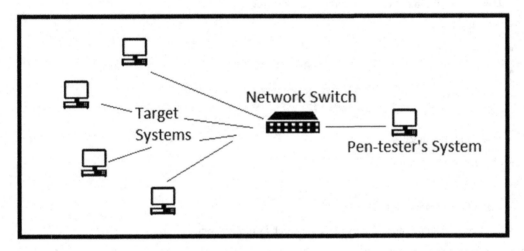

Figure 7-3. *Internal penetration testing, with the attacker attacking from a system located in the internal private network/LAN*

Black Box Penetration Testing

In *black-box* penetration testing, the tester has no prior knowledge about the target. This closely simulates the real world attacks and reduces the false positives. This type of testing requires extensive research and information gathering on the target system/network. It typically consumes more time, effort, and cost to perform a black box penetration test.

Gray-Box Penetration Testing

In *gray-box* penetration testing, the tester has limited or partial knowledge about the target infrastructure, security mechanisms in place, and the communication channels that are to be tested. It simulates real-world attacks that might be performed by an internal person or an external attacker with limited knowledge or privileges on the target system.

White-Box Penetration Testing

In *white-box* penetration testing, the tester has complete in-depth knowledge about the target infrastructure, security mechanisms in place and the communication channels that are to be tested. This type of testing helps simulate an attack that might be performed by an insider who has full knowledge and privileges on the target system.

Announced Testing

In this type of testing, the IT staff, the network team, and the management team of the organization are informed about the schedule of the testing so everyone is aware when the testing will be initiated.

Unannounced Testing

In this type of testing, the IT staff and network and support teams are not informed about any scheduled testing. Only the top management is aware of the test schedule. Such testing helps determine the responsiveness of the IT and support staff in case of a security attack.

Automated Testing

Because penetration testing involves many tasks and the attack surface area is also complex at times, some organizations prefer to use tools for automated penetration testing. They simply run the tool against their infrastructure at regular intervals and then share the reports with concerned teams to address the issues. However, automated testing has its own limitations. The tool will only check for predefined vulnerabilities and is likely to report more false positives. It also cannot review architecture and system integration from a security perspective. However, it is suitable for scanning multiple targets repeatedly and to complement manual testing.

Manual Testing

In manual testing, the tester uses his own expertise and skills in order to penetrate the target system. It has less chance of producing false positives. The tests are performed in a more controlled manner. The tester can also perform reviews of architecture and other procedural aspects in consultation with respective teams. For a holistic security testing, it is best to use a combination of automated and manual testing.

The Penetration Testing Lifecycle

Penetration testing is not just about randomly running a few tools and generating reports. It's a complete process that involves multiple phases and requires active participation from all the stakeholders (Figure 7-4). The following sections explain a typical penetration testing lifecycle starting from the engagement with customer to the delivery of executive reports.

Figure 7-4. *Phases of penetration testing*

The Pre-Attack Phase

The pre-attack phase consists of several important activities, including defining and agreeing upon the rules of engagement, thoroughly understanding the client requirements, finalizing the test scope, signing agreements and contracts, and then beginning to gather information about the target network.

1. **Define the rules of engagement**: Before initiating any new assignment or contract, the parties involved must mutually agree on terms, conditions, and rules that will secure the interests of both parties during execution of the assignment. Similarly, before starting a penetration testing project, it is necessary to agree upon common rules of engagement that will empower the pen-tester to freely execute the tests.

2. **Understand customer requirements**: Before initiating the pen test, it is important to understand the customer requirements. The pen-tester must clearly understand what the customer expects from the test. Certain customers might require the pen-testing to be performed only during nonbusiness hours. Customers might also have specifications about who should be kept involved and informed throughout the testing as well as for final reporting. All such customer requirements must be captured and documented formally.

3. **Create a checklist of testing requirements**: Before starting the actual penetration test, it can be helpful to interact with the client and develop a checklist or summary of existing security controls that have been implemented. The tester should determine what policies or standards the organization follows, and whether the organization requires an assessment of its physical security as well. Does the organization use any technologies like BYOD (bring your own device), and is that to be tested for vulnerabilities? Floating such a questionnaire and recording responses in the form of a checklist will better help the pen-tester in finalizing the scope of the penetration test and meet the customer requirements more accurately.

4. **Define and finalize pen-testing scope**: Scoping is an extremely important part of the penetration testing assignment. If scoping is done improperly, it can lead to disputes in later phases of the test. It is essential to discuss, plan, and review the scope of testing with the customer and explicitly describe it in writing in the contract. The scope typically involves which assets and processes are to be tested and how they are going to be tested (internally or externally, and so on).

5. **Sign penetration testing contract**: Once all the requirements and scope have been agreed upon and finalized with the customer, it is important to sign a formal legal contract with all the terms and conditions defined clearly. This will help safeguard the interests of both the penetration tester and the customer.

6. **Sign non-disclosure agreement (NDA)**: The results that are generated from a penetration test may contain extremely sensitive and confidential customer data. It is extremely crucial for a pen-tester to keep these results and findings confidential and not leak them anywhere. Thus it is essential that the pen-tester signs a confidentiality or non-disclosure agreement (NDA) to assure the customer that its information will be treated confidentially and securely.

7. **Information gathering, reconnaissance (active or passive):** Abraham Lincoln once said, "Give me six hours to chop down a tree and I will spend the first four sharpening the axe." This famous quote applies in penetration testing as well. In order to perform a successful penetration test, the pen-tester must first spend quality time gathering meaningful information about the target. The information may include the following:

- IP range

- Live hosts

- Website registrant details

- DNS and mail server information

- Operating systems used

- Personnel contact information

- Any other leads or pieces of information that would further help building an attack

Reconnaissance can be classified into two types:

- **Active reconnaissance**: In active reconnaissance, the attacker sends actual packets/datagrams/probes to the target system or network to gather information. This may include ping scans, SYN scans, operating system enumerations, banner grabbing, and so on. However, such type of reconnaissance activity may raise an alarm and could be detected easily.

- **Passive reconnaissance**: In passive reconnaissance, the pen-tester tries to gather as much as information about the target system from publicly available sources, like the organization's website or social media. The pen-tester doesn't use his tools to send packets/probes to the target organization, thus avoiding any direct contact, which might raise an alert.

The Attack Phase

Once the pen-test project is kicked off by completing the activities in the pre-attack phase, it is time to find any vulnerabilities and exploit the weaknesses found in the target system. This mainly involves enumerating the devices, acquiring the targets, and escalating privileges.

- **Perimeter testing**: The network perimeter mainly includes devices like firewalls, intrusion detection systems, intrusion prevention systems, and access control gateways. A pen-tester needs to use various techniques to evade and bypass these perimeter security devices and get inside the target network. The pen-tester can craft special IP packets (manipulating the TCP flags) and send them to the target network to test the strength of firewall rules. A certain level of probing may also reveal which protocols are allowed and which are restricted. The IDS and IPS devices must also be tested, by passing malicious traffic.

- **Enumerating devices**: Device enumeration includes creating a device inventory with all the necessary parameters like the name of each device, its IP address, MAC address, physical location, and the like. This can be done using tools like NMAP, which scans the entire network and creates a network or host map. This information can be later used to verify and identify any fake, unauthorized, or rogue device that might exist in the network. Figure 7-5 is a sample network topology graph generated from an NMAP scan.

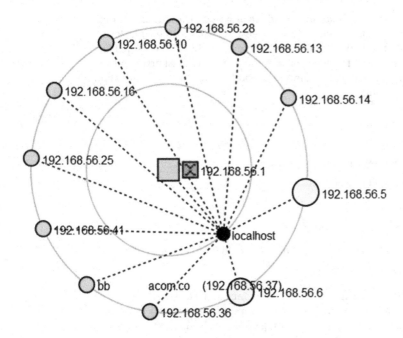

Figure 7-5. *Graph showing live hosts in the network*

- **Acquiring targets**: This phase is more intrusive, and the pen tester tries to gain access to all possible devices that were enumerated earlier. The tester makes use of manual techniques as well as automated scanning tools to break into the target systems. Once the pen-tester has access to the target system, the next step is to determine which resources can be accessed. The resources might contain company-confidential data, trade secrets, employee data, payroll data, or any other sensitive information.

- **Escalating privileges**: Once the pen-tester gets basic access to the target, they also need to aim for privilege escalation. The ultimate objective here is to get access to the administrator or root level user so as to gain the maximum possible control over the target system. The pen-tester may use various techniques, like a brute-force attack or existing system vulnerabilities, to escalate the privileges.

- **Execute and implant**: In this phase the pen-tester tries to execute arbitrary code on the target system and also attempts to implant back doors for future compromise. Techniques include exploiting buffer overflows or any such vulnerabilities found in the target system. The pen-tester will then also test whether he can manipulate the audit log to clear his tracks and get away without being noticed.

The Post-Attack Phase

Once all the tests have been performed on the target systems or network, it is necessary to clean and restore the systems. This phase usually involves the following tasks:

- **Removing uploaded files**: Many times testers upload malicious files, scripts, payloads, or executables on the target system for the purpose of exploitation. It is necessary to remove all such uploaded files so that they don't act as a backdoor to any unauthorized users thereafter.

- **Cleaning Registry entries**: Many exploits on Windows systems make modifications in the Registry. It is necessary to clean out such malicious Registry entries. The best way is to take a snapshot of the Registry before starting the tests and then restore the Registry to that snapshot after completion of all tests.

- **Removing tools and exploits**: The entire penetration testing process involves using many tools. It's quite possible that the tester may have uploaded a set of tools on a particular system within the target network. In such a scenario, it's necessary to remove all the tools once testing is complete.

- **Restoring network**: For testing specific scenarios, the network policies or the Access Control Lists (ACLs) may have been modified. All such modifications must be restored to their original state.

- **Analyzing results**: The process of penetration testing involves numerous tests, either automated or manual. All these tests generate a lot of output data. It is essential to analyze the result data from all the tests, remove false positives, and organize the results in a structured manner.

- **Presenting the findings report**: All the effort that is put into the penetration test will go in vain if a good report isn't prepared and presented to relevant stakeholders. The report must be tailored to the stakeholders and must contain an executive summary, detailed findings, proof-of-concept (PoC) wherever applicable, and fix recommendations. The report must contain sufficient information for stakeholders to act upon the issues and must be easy to understand.

In this section we had an overview of various phases of penetration testing. An important aspect to consider throughout these phases is audit logging. It is essential that the pen-tester enable audit log for all the tests performed during these phases. This will not only help the pen-tester in preparing a better test report but will also help to differentiate between the test traffic and any actual attack traffic that might have been triggered during the pen-test. Most of the tools used for pen-testing produce audit and debug logs. These logs can be preserved and used later during final reporting.

False Positives and False Negatives

Penetration testing involves use of many automated vulnerability scanning tools, which generate vulnerability reports. However, these tools have their own limitations and at times the results from these tools may be incorrect. Such cases require manual verification whether the reported vulnerability really exists or not. Following are the two terms widely used in this regard:

- **False positive**: A false positive means a vulnerability has been incorrectly identified. That is, the target system is not vulnerable, but the vulnerability scanner has still reported it to be vulnerable.

- **False negative**: A false negative means a vulnerability exists in the target system but has not been identified by the vulnerability scanner.

Summary

The following key points summarize the important concepts that we have learned throughout this chapter:

- *Security assessment* is a broad term that can be further classified into security audits, vulnerability assessments, and penetration testing.

- A penetration test simulates the methods and techniques used by real-world attackers to gain unauthorized access to an organization's system.

- There are various types of penetration testing, like internal or external, black box/gray box/white box, and announced or unannounced.

- Reconnaissance can be classified into two types: active and passive.

- It is essential to sign a non-disclosure agreement (NDA) before starting the penetration test. This ensures that the company-confidential information isn't leaked during or after the testing.

- At the end of the test, it is important to prepare a report with sufficient information for the stakeholders to understand and fix the vulnerabilities.

Do-It-Yourself (DIY) Exercises

1. Download and install Zenmap for network scanning. Explore various switches of NMAP.

2. Download and install the community edition of Nessus and scan localhost for vulnerabilities.

3. Read the Penetration Testing Standard located at `http://www.pentest-standard.org`.

Test Your Knowledge: Sample Questions

1. Which of the following should be included in the scope of penetration testing?

   a. DNS server

   b. Mail server

   c. Communication links

   d. All of the above

2. Which of the following most closely simulates the actions of a real world attacker/hacker?

   a. Vulnerability assessment

   b. Security audit

   c. Penetration testing

   d. None of the above

3. Which of the following techniques could be used to test a firewall?

   a. Send specially crafted packets by manipulating TCP headers and flags

   b. Perform brute force attack

   c. Perform SQL injection attack

   d. None of the above

4. Which of the following is a test wherein the pen-tester has partial knowledge about the target system/network?

   a. Black box testing

   b. White box testing

   c. Gray box testing

   d. Blue box testing

5. Which of the following is one of the important documents to be signed before the penetration test to safeguard interest of the concerned parties?

   a. Legal agreement

   b. Service level agreement

   c. Non-disclosure agreement (NDA)

   d. All of the above

6. Sending a probe to the target system using a ping scan is a form of which type of reconnaissance?

   a. Active reconnaissance

   b. Passive reconnaissance

   c. Both a and b

   d. None of the above

7. A system is infected with a virus, but the anti-virus software is not able to detect it. This is an example of:

   a. False positive

   b. False negative

CHAPTER 8

Information Gathering

Before planning an attack on the target system or network, it is very important to have detailed information about the target system. This information includes software versions, type of operating system installed, a list of active services, a list of user accounts, and so on. This information helps plan and build or prevent further attacks on the target system. This chapter introduces various footprinting and enumeration techniques that are useful in gathering vital information about the target system.

Key Topics   Types and importance of footprinting, enumeration, and common tools for enumeration

---

What is Footprinting?

Footprinting is one of the initial stages of the hacking methodology. It is used to collect as much information as possible about the target system and/or network. It involves getting information about the target network topology, performing DNS and WHOIS queries, finding out the versions of remote operating systems and application software, and then consolidating this information to build further attacks.

Before planning for the actual attack on the target network, footprinting gives a wealth of information to the attacker. It helps determine strengths and weaknesses of the target network. It gives information about the critical assets in that target network so that more emphasis can be made on exploiting those. In a way, it helps attacker visualize the security posture of the target network and then plan for the most accurate attack vectors. Without footprinting, the attacker is less likely to succeed with exploitation of the vulnerabilities in the target network.

The following list provides the different types of footprinting:

- **Website footprinting**: This involves getting information about the target website. For example, `http://www.netcraft.com/` is a website that offers rich footprinting services. It can tell you what server and software the target is running along with other details, such as uptime. A Firefox plug-in known as Wappalyzer also gives information about what web server, OS, and other add-ons or plug-ins the target site is running. Figure 8-1 shows a sample output (marked in green boxes) from the Wappalyzer plug-in.

Figure 8-1. *Website footprinting with Wappalyzer*

- Another useful website, `http://www.bulkdachecker.com/url-extractor/`, helps extract all the links in the target website. This further assists in plotting the attack surface and excluding the items that may be out of scope. Figure 8-2 shows the tool results for one of the demo websites.

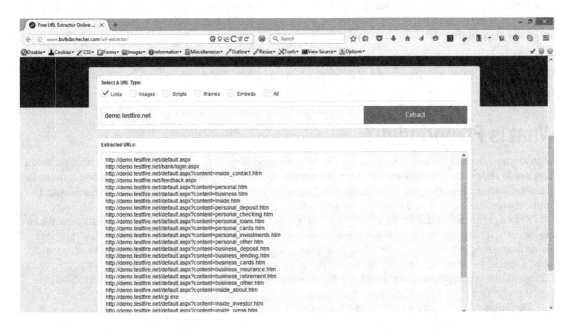

Figure 8-2. *URL extractor for extracting all hyperlinks from the target website*

- **Email footprinting:** This technique involves gathering information about the email recipient by using various tracing and tracking techniques.

  - **Email Tracing:** Every email has two parts, a header and a body. The email header contains technical information, including the mail server used to send the email, timestamps, and so on, and the email body contains the actual message that was sent. The email header can reveal lot of useful information about the sender. For example, the site `http://www.traceemail.com/trace-email-header.html` allows users to trace an email just by copy-pasting the email header into the Trace utility (Figure 8-3).

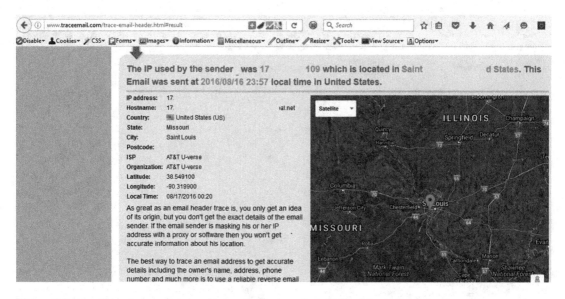

Figure 8-3. *Email tracing service showing location where the email originated*

- **Email Tracking**: This technique involves sending an email to a recipient in order to track the location and other details of the target user. For example, www.readnotify.com is one such website that allows users to track emails sent through this service. It works as follows:

  - A user sends an email to the target recipient using readnotify.

  - The receiver receives the email and opens it.

  - As soon as the receiver opens the email for reading, the sender receives a notification that the mail was opened along with location and other details.

- **Competitive intelligence**: Competitive intelligence is a methodology used by businesses to gather and analyze information about products and customers of rival companies. This information is then used to formulate better business strategies. For example, the site www.sec.gov/edgar.shtml gives lot of interesting information about various registered companies.

- **WHOIS search**: Querying the WHOIS database returns the domain registrant information. To find out registrant information for any website, one can use https://whois.icann.org . For example, a WHOIS query for demo.testfire.net triggered the results in Figure 8-4.

Figure 8-4. *WHOIS search query result for* `demo.testfire.net`

- **Footprinting using Google**: Google is one of the most popular and widely used search engines. However, in addition to its basic search function, it offers several advanced search operators that help narrow down the search results to extract the exact information needed. Table **8-1** lists some of the advanced Google search operators useful for footprinting.

Table 8-1. *Some Useful Advanced Google Search Operators*

Operator	Example	Description
Site:	Site:example.com	Returns results only from the specified domain example.com.
Allinurl:	Allinurl:secret.txt	Lists all URLs that contain the string "secret.txt".
Allintitle:	Allintitle: index of	Lists all web pages that contain the string "index of" in their title tag.
Cache:	Cache:example.com	Displays the version of example.com when it was last visited by Google.
Filetype:	Filetype:pdf	Searches the target only for "pdf" files.

For more interesting Google search operators, visit `https://www.exploit-db.com/google-hacking-database/`

- **DNS footprinting**: DNS servers contain a wealth of information in the form of internal IP addresses, host names, and pointers to other servers. This information can be extracted to build a further attack. The site `www.dnsstuff.com` offers various tools for interrogating the remote DNS server.

- **People search and social networking sites**: There are many free and publicly available sites that let you search for people. Depending on the type of site, you can get personal as well as professional information about the target person. Facebook, one of the most popular social networking sites, easily gives out personal information like pictures, locations visited, topics of interests and so on, while the professional social networking platform Linkedin gives information about various organizations the target person has worked for and his professional skills. This information base can be quite useful to build a social engineering attack and increase the probability of compromise. Figure 8-5 shows another popular people search engine known as Pipl.

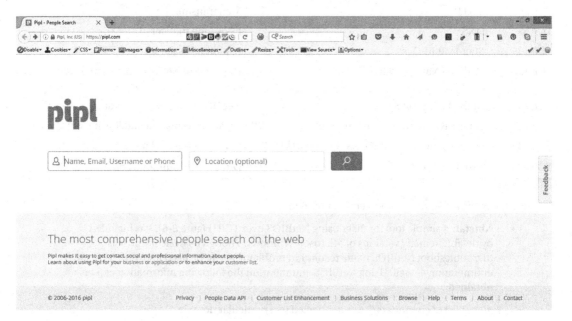

Figure 8-5. *Pipl search engine for finding people over the Internet*

- **Searching devices with Shodan:** The Internet is not just a place where only individual computers and systems are connected. Today's Internet is a complex network of things and devices. Industrial control systems are also often interconnected over the Internet. Shodan is a special-purpose search engine for security enthusiasts that helps find devices, passwords, databases, webcams, and so on over the Internet using specialized queries. Shodan is extremely easy to use and is located at `https://www.shodan.io`.

- **Maltego search engine**: Maltego (`https://www.paterva.com`) is an advanced search tool that searches for the subject across the Internet and creates a relationship graph between the searched entities.

113

What is Enumeration?

Enumeration is a process of retrieving information like usernames, default credentials, host names, network shares, and services from the target system. This is done by creating a connection with the target system and then making relevant queries to extract the required information. This information creates a solid base on which a further attack can be built. Common services and ports for enumeration are listed in Table 8-2.

Table 8-2. *Common TCP Ports for Enumeration*

Port	Service	Enumeration Output
TCP 25	SMTP	Mail transmission
TCP 53	DNS	DNS zone transfer
TCP 135	Microsoft RPC	Exploit message services
TCP 137	NetBIOS Name Service	Database of NetBIOS names for hosts and corresponding IP addresses
TCP 139	NetBIOS Session Service	NetBIOS sessions, shared data
TCP 161	Simple Network Management Protocol (SNMP)	Device information and logging data
TCP 389	Lightweight Directory Access Protocol (LDAP)	Centralized user database
TCP 445	SMB Over TCP	Direct host communication

The following are some common enumeration tools:

- **Nbtstat**: A simple tool for diagnosing NetBIOS over TCP (Figure 8-6). It is included by default in many versions of Microsoft Windows. Though its basic purpose is to troubleshoot NetBIOS name resolution problems, it can be used for NetBIOS enumeration as well. Using NetBIOS enumeration the following information can be obtained:

  - A list of computers/hosts connected in a particular domain

  - A list of shares on individual hosts

  - Domain policies

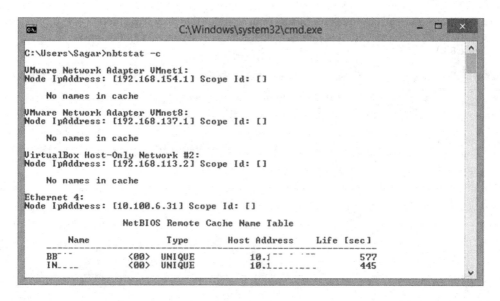

Figure 8-6. *NetBIOS enumeration with nbtstat*

- **NMAP**: NMAP is the most popular and widely used port scanning tool. Apart from port scanning, it also enumerates services, detects operating system versions, and creates a network topology. It also offers advanced options for stealth scanning, IDS evasion, and custom scripting. Figure 8-7 shows ZenMAP, which is a GUI to NMAP.

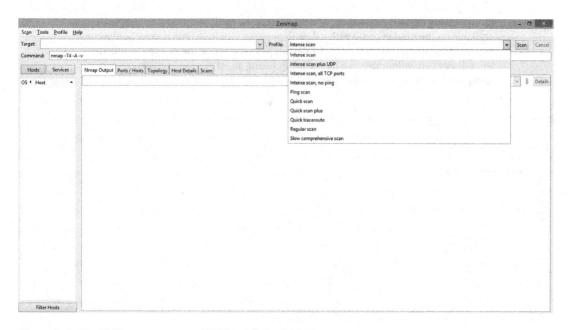

Figure 8-7. *ZenMAP port scanner, a GUI front end to NMAP*

- **Superscan**: Superscan is another useful tool from MacAfee that does IP scanning, host and service discovery, port scanning, zone transfers, and Windows enumeration (Figure 8-8).

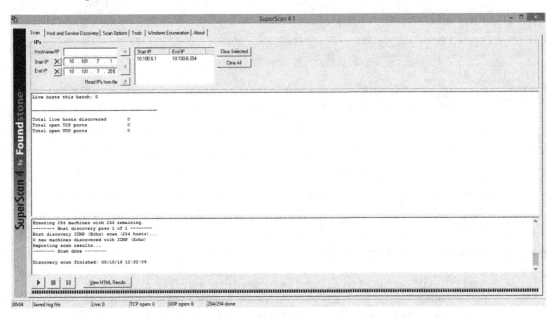

Figure 8-8. *SuperScan tool for network host and service discovery*

- **Enumerating default passwords**: Almost all devices, equipment, and appliances available on the market come with a default password for first-time access. Sometimes an administrator forgets to change the default password once the device is configured. Such devices are vulnerable to a password-guessing attack. Default passwords can easily be enumerated using the website `www.defaultpassword.com` (Figure 8-9).

Figure 8-9. *Default password list for software and appliances from different vendors*

- **The Finger command**: Finger is a commonly used Linux/Unix utility for finding out information about computer users. By querying with Finger, one can get login name, full name, home directory, shell path, last login details, and so on.

- **Netscantools Pro**: Netscantools Pro is a suite of utilities for network footprinting and enumeration. It offers various services like ARP scan, OS fingerprinting, and SMB enumeration, WHOIS, Packet Generator and Flooder, and others (Figure 8-10).

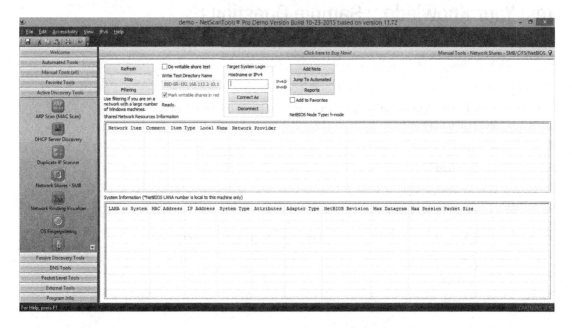

Figure 8-10. *Netscantools Pro tool for network footprinting and enumeration*

Summary

Following are the key takeaways from the chapter:

- *Footprinting* is one of the initial stages of the hacking methodology and is used to collect information about the target system and/or network.

- Website footprinting, email footprinting, and DNS footprinting are some of the common types of footprinting.

- *Enumeration* is a process of retrieving information such as usernames, default credentials, host names, network shares, and services from the target system.

- NMAP, Superscan and Netscantools Pro are some of the tools used for host and service discovery and network enumeration.

Do-It-Yourself (DIY) Exercises

1. Explore the website www.netcraft.com for website footprinting.

2. Trace the origin of any email of your choice.

3. Find the registrant details of any domain of your choice using WHOIS search.

4. Explore various advanced Google search operators discussed in this chapter.

5. Download and install ZenMAP and explore various options for network enumeration.

Test Your Knowledge: Sample Questions

1. Email tracing is same as email tracking. True or false?

    a. True

    b. False

2. Which of the following Google search operator limits the search only to a particular domain?

    a. Allintitle:

    b. Allinurl:

    c. Site:

    d. None of the above.

3. Which of the following is a utility for enumerating NetBIOS shares?

    a. Netstat

    b. Nbtstat

    c. Nslookup

    d. ps

4. Which of the following is used to find domain registration information?

    a. Finger

    b. WHOIS

    c. PING

    d. All of the above.

5. Which of the following search engines is used to find devices over the Internet?

    a. WHOIS

    b. Netcraft

    c. Shodan

    d. Bing

CHAPTER 9

Hacking Basics

Hacking into systems involves a methodological approach which consists of various tools and techniques. This chapter covers the basics of the hacking lifecycle, starting from cracking the passwords to gain entry into remote systems up through covering one's tracks and traces before exiting from the compromised system.

■ **Key Topics** Password cracking techniques, keyloggers, Trojans, viruses, worms, rootkits, social engineering, privilege escalation, denial of service attack, botnet, alternate data streams, steganography, covering tracks.

Password-Cracking Techniques

Various password-cracking techniques can be used to recover passwords from different systems. Attackers often use these techniques to gain unauthorized access to the target system. When password-cracking techniques are successful, it is most often due to weak password policy on the target system. People often use simple passwords, dictionary words, and so on, making their systems vulnerable to password cracking.

Password complexity is a very important factor in deciding the strength of a password. Following are some of the rules that help to generate a complex and hard-to-crack password:

- A combination of alphabetical letters, digits, and special characters

- Both uppercase and lowercase characters

- A minimum length of 8 characters

- Not allowing the password to be the same as the username

- Restricting the use of trivial words like dictionary words

Following are some of the commonly used password-cracking techniques:

- **Dictionary attack**: This is the most commonly used technique. Here the password cracker loads a dictionary of words and checks each and every word for a correct password match. This attack succeeds if the password of the target system is one of the dictionary words fed by the password cracker. There are regional and language-specific dictionaries easily available on the Internet.

- **Brute force attack**: A brute force attack is used to crack a password that is not a dictionary word. In this attack, the password cracker tries all possible permutations and combinations of a given character set to match against the password. This attack is certainly resource-intensive and time-consuming.

- **Hybrid attack**: A hybrid attack is built further upon the dictionary attack. People often have the habit of adding characters or digits to trivial words. For example, "apple" is a dictionary word, and a user might choose "apple123" as her password. A hybrid attack creates such trivial combinations based on dictionary words and then tries to crack the password.

- **Syllable attack**: A syllable attack is a combination of brute force and dictionary attacks.

- **Rule-based attack**: A rule-based attack is used when the attacker has some knowledge about the password. For example, the attacker might know that the password is not more than six characters and contains two digits. This might help the password cracker to limit the permutations and combinations and hence crack the password in less time.

- **Rainbow tables**: A rainbow table is another advanced password cracking technique, which precomputes password hashes for all the permutations and combinations of a given character set. Because all the computation work is done in advance, the password cracking is significantly faster than the other traditional methods for password recovery. There are a couple of free online services like `http://md5cracker.org/` that allow attackers to crack hashes using rainbow tables.

- **Distributed password recovery**: Distributed password recovery uses multiple computing systems in parallel to crack a password instead of a single system. Since multiple systems or a complete network of systems are involved in the cracking process, it produces the result much faster.

- **Non-technical attacks**: These attacks involve password guessing, dumpster diving (searching trash bins for papers that might have passwords written on them), shoulder surfing (standing behind the victim and watching him type his password), social engineering, and so on.

Keyloggers

A *keylogger* is a type of malware that is commonly used to steal passwords and pins. The keylogger hides itself on the target system and silently captures all the keys pressed (through the keyboard) on the system. The key-log is then secretly sent to the attacker using mail, FTP, or similar communication media. The key-log may contain passwords, pin numbers, credit card and online payment information, mail communications, and chat messages keyed by the victim. Some keyloggers even take a screenshot of the victim's desktop and send it across to the attacker at regular intervals. Following are some of the types of keyloggers:

- **BIOS embedded**: This type of keylogger embeds and hides itself by modifying the BIOS of the target system. It basically modifies the part of firmware that handles keyboard actions.

- **Keylogger keyboard**: The attacker can replace the normal keyboard on the victim system with this special-purpose keylogger keyboard, which looks exactly the same as the original one. However it has its own internal memory which it uses to secretly store all the key logs typed through that keyboard.

- **External keyloggers**: These come as small connectors which can fit it the PS/2 or serial ports where the normal keyboard is connected. They intercept and store all the keylogs passing through them.

- **Software keyloggers**: These are the most commonly used keyloggers, which are implanted into the target system just like any other malware. Once active, they silently capture all the keys typed and send them to the remote attacker.

Trojans

A Trojan is a malicious and harmful piece of code hidden inside a genuine and innocent-looking program or application. Trojans are activated upon certain user actions and activities, and once active, the Trojan gives the attacker full access to the victim's system. The attacker can get all passwords stored on the compromised system, read confidential documents, modify or delete files, access a microphone or webcam, access a printer (if installed), and even format the entire hard drive. An attacker can simply send a game or a music player embedded with a Trojan to the victim. The victim would install and run the application without any suspicion, activating the Trojan silently in the background. The Trojan would now listen to commands remotely from the attacker. Typically, a Trojan uses one of the following communication paths for its malicious activities:

- **Overt channel**: An overt channel is a genuine and legitimate path for communication between computer systems. For example, a chat messenger would use an overt channel for communication.

- **Covert channel**: A covert channel is a secret backdoor type of channel for communicating with a remote system. It violates the security policy. Trojans make use of covert channels for communicating with the attacker. Some Trojans even modify an overt channel for malicious communication.

Types of Trojans

There are many types of Trojans based on the activities and functions they perform. Some of the common ones are:

- **Command-shell Trojans**: This type of Trojan gives the attacker remote command-line access to the victim's system. The server component of the Trojan opens up a port for the attacker to connect to. Using the Trojan client, the attacker launches the command shell on the remote system. Netcat is a popular command-line tool that can be maliciously used for remote control.

- **Document Trojans**: Most antivirus programs detect malicious activities when an executable (.exe file) is launched. To evade and bypass the antivirus protection, some Trojans hide or embed themselves in documents like Word files or Excel spreadsheets. When the victim opens such maliciously crafted documents, the Trojan is triggered and gives remote access to the attacker.

- **Email Trojans**: Email Trojans help the attacker gain control of the victim's system by sending commands over email messages. The server component of the Trojan actively listens to and monitors all email communication. The attacker sends commands to the Trojan over email, and the Trojan responds accordingly. Remote-by-mail is a type of email Trojan that allows an attacker to send commands and control the system remotely.

- **Botnet Trojans**: Attackers use botnet Trojans to infect a large number of systems and then use all of the compromised systems at once to attack a particular victim system. This is often used to launch attacks like the distributed denial of service attack.

Viruses

A virus is a type of malicious program or code that self-replicates with the intent of modifying, deleting, or permanently damaging the infected system. Viruses are easily propagated through file downloads from unknown sources, email attachments, infected USB drives, and so on. Viruses often use various techniques like self-encryption and polymorphism to remain undetected by antivirus software.

Following are the stages you might find in a typical virus lifecycle:

- **Design and development**: The author or creator of the virus does research on latest security trends and accordingly designs and develops virus code that can cause severe impact.

- **Infection and replication**: Once the virus is developed, it starts replicating itself on the target system and tries to bring as many systems as possible under its infection.

- **Trigger and launch**: The virus code might have certain conditions upon which it is triggered and launched. There might be certain user activities and events that launch the virus on the infected system. For example, many viruses spread when user plugs the USB drive and double clicks some of the folder containing malicious code.

- **Detection**: Because the virus causes unwanted modifications or damage to the infected system, it is detected by either the antivirus program or the system administrators.

- **Anti-virus signature development**: Most of the antivirus programs have predefined signature and heuristic capabilities to detect any unwanted malicious activity on the system. However, modern-day viruses use advanced techniques to hide themselves from antivirus tools. To remove and disinfect such viruses, antivirus companies need to research and develop new signatures and removal techniques.

- **Eradication**: Once the antivirus software has a removal solution in place, it is distributed to all the users in the vform of a signature update. Once the antivirus is updated, it can eradicate the virus from the system and attempt to clean the infected files.

Types of Viruses

There are many types of viruses, based on the actions they perform. Some of the common types of viruses are:

- **System/boot-sector virus**: This type of virus infects the boot sector of the disk. The virus is triggered when the operating system boots up. The virus replaces or modifies the master boot record (MBR) in order to infect the system.

- **File virus**: File viruses are quite common and infect system executable files like .exe, .com, .bat, and so on. Such viruses are most likely to cause permanent damage to the executable files.

- **Macro virus**: Macro viruses infect and spread through Microsoft Word and Excel documents and spreadsheets. The virus code is written in the form of a macro using Visual Basic script and is triggered upon opening the infected file or other custom actions.

- **Polymorphic virus**: Antivirus programs detect viruses based on either predefined signatures or behavior patterns. To bypass the antivirus detection, certain viruses change their code or their behavior each time they run. The virus contains a polymorphic engine to change itself frequently to avoid detection.

Computer Worms

Worms are similar to viruses,; however, they tend to self-replicate and spread aggressively on as many systems as possible with the intent of consuming computing resources (storage, bandwidth, processing, and so on). Some worms even open a backdoor for the attacker and drop payloads for further compromise.

Rootkits

Rootkits are a special type of malicious program that hides itself by making kernel-level changes in the operating system. They modify or replace certain low-level system calls in order to remain undetected from the antivirus software. Removing a rootkit from an infected system is much harder than removing a virus or a worm. It may require replacing the operating system or the firmware.

Online Malware Analysis

There are several options available from multiple vendors for choosing an antivirus program for a system. It may happen that a particular virus might be detected by antivirus of only a particular vendor. In that case users using antivirus tools from other vendors might be at risk. This is where some of the online malware scanning services come handy. A service called VirusTotal has multiple antivirus engines (from different vendors) running at the back end. When a user submits a file to VirusTotal, it is scanned simultaneously by multiple antivirus scanners, hence increasing the probability of detection if infected. Figure 9-1 shows the results of a file scan by VirusTotal.

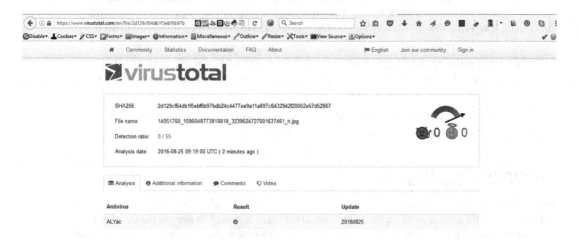

Figure 9-1. *Online tool Virus Total scanning the uploaded file with multiple anti-virus engines*

What Is Social Engineering?

Social engineering is the deceptive art of engaging and communicating with people in order to retrieve confidential information. Most people are unaware that information they possess is indeed valuable. Social engineers use various tricks to convince their victims to give out sensitive information. In a very simple social engineering attack, an attacker would call his victim, pretend to be a bank official, and then ask the victim for his credit card number and PIN. The victim would give away the details, believing the call was really from an authorized bank official. All the information that is gathered through various footprinting techniques is very useful in building successful social engineering attacks. It is often said that humans are the weakest link in the security chain. Social engineers take advantage of this fact to exploit human behavior and extract confidential information. Social engineering can be quite difficult to detect, and there is no special hardware or software that could completely prevent it from occurring. User awareness is the only solution for mitigating social engineering risks.

Following are the various phases of social engineering:

- **Research and information gathering**: This is the first phase of a social engineering attack. The attacker does comprehensive research on the target organization through various information sources. Social networking sites, job boards, and people search engines give out a lot of valuable information.

- **Choosing the victim/target**: Based on the information collected, the attacker then analyzes and chooses the most vulnerable person who could reveal sensitive information to engage with.

- **Establish trust relationship**: Once the victim has been chosen, the attacker communicates with the victim through various ways, like instant messaging, email, or a direct call. The attacker claims to be someone the victim can relate to and trust.

- **Exploit the relationship**: The attacker now tries to exploit the established trust relationship. By engaging the victim in deceptive talk, the attacker tries to extract as much as information as possible.

Following are some types of social engineering:

- **Human based**: This type of social engineering involves human interaction. The attacker impersonates an important role like a technician or a senior executive and tries to establish either trust or fear to further exploit and extract information from the victim.

- **Computer-based**: This type of social engineering involves sending fake, spoofed, and phishing mails to the victim, sending chat messages, and so on to deceive and extract the required information.

- **Mobile based**: This type of social engineering involves the use of malicious apps, fake applications, and sending spoofed SMS.

Privilege Escalation

An attacker often gets unauthorized access to the target system through a nonadminstrative (lower privileged) or local service account user. Once the access is established, however, the attacker tries to escalate or increase the privilege level to gain better control of the system. An attacker can perform privilege escalation by exploiting vulnerabilities and flaws in design, through programming errors and misconfigurations in the operating system. Buffer overflow vulnerabilities are most commonly exploited for escalating privileges.

Denial of Service Attack

As the name suggests, a Denial of Service (DoS) attack is an attack that restricts, limits, or entirely blocks legitimate and authorized users from accessing the system resources. The attacker uses various techniques to stop the target system from functioning so that all users connected to that system are affected. A very simple example of a DoS attack is when an attacker tries different credentials and the system locks the user account of a legitimate user because of frequent unsuccessful attempts. This would restrict the legitimate user from accessing her account until the account is unlocked again. Other common techniques include flooding the servers with a huge number of requests so that they stop responding to any genuine requests. Some years ago, an attack named "Ping of Death" was quite popular. This attack involved sending too many Ping requests to the target system until it crashes and stops responding. However, modern systems have become quite robust and are not prone to such Ping attacks. To overcome this, attackers today use newer techniques like Distributed Denial of Service attack (DDoS). This involves using multiple systems to attack a single system. Imagine thousands of systems generating huge traffic targeted toward a single system; this would cause a crash and disruption in service. To illustrate how DoS attacks work, let's consider the following example of a SYN Flood attack (recall that in Chapter 3 we saw how a TCP 3-way handshake works):

1. Host A (the attacker) sends a SYN packet to host B (the victim).

2. Host B sends a SYN+ACK to host A and waits for a response.

3. Host A doesn't send an ACK to host B, and Host B keeps waiting for the connection to complete.

4. Host A sends multiple such half-open connection requests to host B.

5. This fills the connection queue of host B with half-open requests. Hence, host B cannot accept any new genuine requests from any other host until its connection queue is freed.

Another variant of the DoS attack is known as a *Permanent Denial of Service attack (PDoS)*. The DoS and DDoS attacks that we have discussed so far exploit flaws in a software application. Hence, the affected service can be easily restored by resetting or restarting the application. In a PDoS attack, however, the attacker sends a malicious and corrupt firmware file to the victim. When the victim downloads and installs the firmware, it permanently damages the hardware and requires the victim to completely replace the hardware in order to restore the service.

Botnet

We have already discussed how DDoS attacks work. A DDoS attack requires multiple systems to attack the target system simultaneously. A botnet is nothing but a group of systems controlled by an attacker to perform a DDoS attack. The botnet has a simple client-server architecture. The attacker exploits some of the local system vulnerabilities to install the botnet client on as many systems as possible. Then, using the master server, the attacker commands all of the clients to attack a particular target at a particular moment. The clients are usually located at different geographical locations across the world. Once the attacker instructs the botnet clients to attack, a huge amount of traffic is generated and the target system quickly runs out of resources and bandwidth, resulting in denial of service to its legitimate users.

Alternate Data Streams

An *Alternate data stream* is the technique of attaching data to a file on an NTFS file system. It is a method used to hide data. The master file table of the NTFS partition has a list of all data streams attached to a particular file, along with their physical location on disk. Content hidden using this technique would not be visible openly to anyone but would require special and explicit knowledge to reveal the hidden content. Attaching hidden content to an existing file does not modify the functionality or size of the original file. Following are the steps to hide data using alternate data streams:

1. Open the command prompt.

2. Type `notepad newfile.txt:hiddent.txt`.

3. Type some text, save the file, and exit.

4. Check the file size of `newfile.txt`; it should be 0 bytes.

5. The file `hidden.txt` has been attached to `newfile.txt` and remains hidden.

While the file `hidden.txt` won't be visible through the command prompt or Windows Explorer, special-purpose tools like StreamArmor can easily detect all alternate data streams present on the system (Figure 9-2).

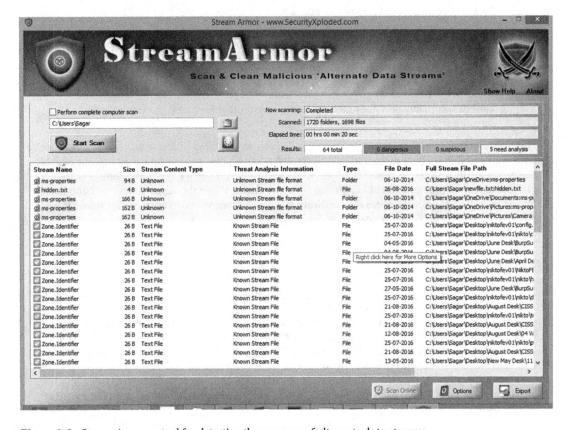

Figure 9-2. StreamArmor, a tool for detecting the presence of alternate data streams

Steganography

Steganography is set of techniques for concealing a message or data inside another message or data file. This technique is primarily used for maintaining confidentiality of the data. Only the parties that are involved in the steganography and have the appropriate key can reveal the hidden message; all others can never suspect its presence. The most common technique used in steganography is hiding the message within an image or a graphic file. The message is hidden inside the image in such a way that there is no change in appearance of the image file, and it looks perfectly normal. Steganography works on the simple principle of replacing unused bits in graphic, sound, text, or video files to store and conceal the hidden data.

Following are some typical uses of steganography:

- **Copy prevention**: The digital entertainment industry is always at risk of piracy. Steganography can be used to protect the copyright of media in CD and DVD format.

- **Hiding metadata**: Metadata (data about data) is often used to track geographical location and to restrict unauthorized copying of digital data. Steganography can be used to hide such metadata.

- **Covert communication**: Steganography is most commonly used to covertly send secret messages concealed within an innocent-looking data file.

- **Authenticity testing**: Digital image files are often duplicated using various techniques. Steganography can be effectively used to identify the original image against the fake image.

Figure 9-3 shows an application called S-Tools, which is used to hide information within an image file. It allows the user to simply drag and drop the image file first and then the data file to be hidden within the image.

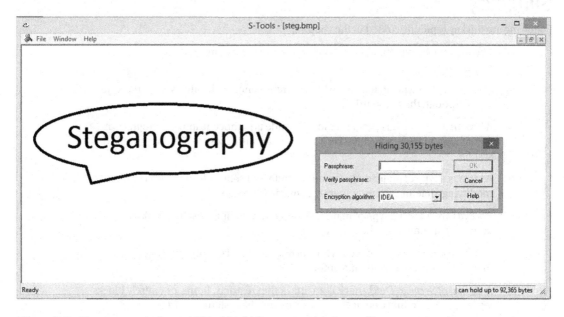

Figure 9-3. *The steganography tool S-Tool for hiding text within image files*

Covering Tracks

You've seen that attackers use various techniques to exploit the vulnerabilities in a target system and compromise the system with maximum privileges. After the compromise is over, however, the attacker would want to clear all traces of how the system was compromised. This will help the attacker remain undetected and may also help in compromising the same system again in the future. The process of clearing the tracks involves some of the following activities:

- Clearing browser history and cache

- Removing any files that were uploaded for the compromise

- Clearing audit and event logs

- Closing ports opened for the compromise

- Stopping the services involved in the compromise

- Restoring the Windows Registry to the point prior to the compromise

- Deleting any user accounts created specifically during the compromise

- Clearing the temp files and recent documents on Windows

- Shredding the payload files and actual evidence, making it impossible to recover

- Tampering with the timestamps of certain system files

Following are some of the tools that are used to clear session data:

- **CCCleaner**: Cleans up temp files, Internet history, Registry entries, cookies, and so on.

- **File Shredder**: Permanently wipes files, making them unrecoverable.

Summary

Following are the key topics discussed in the chapter:

- The *dictionary attack* and *brute-force attack* are most common ways of cracking passwords.

- A *keylogger* is a type of malware which secretly sends to the attacker, all the keys typed through the keyboard.

- A *Trojan* is a malicious program hidden inside an innocent-looking program or application that gives the attacker complete remote access to the compromised system.

- A *virus* is a type of malicious program or code that self-replicates with the intent of modifying, deleting, or permanently damaging the infected system.

- *Rootkits* are a special type of malicious program that hides itself by making kernel-level changes in the operating system.

- *Social engineering* is the deceptive art of engaging and communicating with people in order to retrieve confidential information.

- A *Denial of Service (DoS)* attack is an attack that restricts, limits, or entirely blocks legitimate and authorized users from accessing the system resources.

- *Steganography* is a technique of hiding a message or data within another message or data file.

Test Your Knowledge: Sample Questions

1. Which of the following technique uses precomputed hashes for password cracking?

   a. Dictionary attack

   b. Hybrid attack

   c. Brute force attack

   d. Rainbow table attack

2. Trojans use a covert channel to communicate remotely with the attacker. True or False?

   a. True

   b. False

3. Which of the following viruses spread to Microsoft Office documents like Word and Excel?

   a. File virus

   b. Polymorphic virus

   c. Macro virus

   d. None of the above

4. Which of the following malware types makes kernel-level changes to hide its presence?

   a. Spyware

   b. Worm

   c. Keylogger

   d. Rootkit

CHAPTER 10

■ ■ ■

Web Application Hacking

During the early computing era, hackers and attackers targeted operating systems and infrastructure-level components to compromise the systems. But today's operating systems and other infrastructure components are comparatively mature in terms of security, making it hard for attackers to intrude. With increasing demand for and use of web applications, attackers are now targeting web application vulnerabilities to compromise systems. This chapter introduces common web application vulnerabilities, like SQL injection, cross-site scripting (XSS), cross-site request forgery (CSRF), and others, along with testing methodology and mitigations.

■ **Key Topics** How web applications work, attack vectors, web application flaws, web application hacking methodology, hacking web servers, automated scanning, mitigations.

How Web Applications Work

Using a simple browser, we access many websites and applications on a daily basis. As soon as we enter the URL of the website we want to visit, within a few seconds the web page or the application loads in the browser. We can then interact with it based on its functionality. This process may look straightforward from the end user's perspective, but it involves a lot of communication and processing between various systems at the back-end. Following is a high-level overview of how web applications work:

1. The user enters (in the address bar of the browser) the URL of the website she wishes to visit.

2. The domain name is resolved to an IP address using DNS.

3. The request is received by the web server, which first checks the extension of the requested document (HTML, PHP, ASP, and so on).

4. If the user requested an HTML document, the web server processes the request and responds to the user with the requested HTML page.

5. If the user requested some document with an extension the web server cannot handle, the web server forwards the request to the application server that is capable of processing that particular document.

6. The application server processes the request and may also need to fetch data from the database.

7. Once processing is complete and data is retrieved from the database, the web server responds to the user with the result set.

© Sagar Ajay Rahalkar 2016
S.A. Rahalkar, *Certified Ethical Hacker (CEH) Foundation Guide*, DOI 10.1007/978-1-4842-2325-3_10

Attack Vectors

An attack vector is a path through which an attacker gains unauthorized access to the target system. Once the attacker has access to the target system, he then delivers a payload to exploit vulnerabilities and perform other malicious activities. For example, *SQL injection* is one of the most common attack vectors for web applications. The attacker first finds the web application, which doesn't validate the input. Then he passes specially crafted input containing SQL queries as part of the user input. The SQL query is executed and the attacker gets unauthorized access to sensitive data.

Web Application Flaws

Web applications are often soft targets for attackers who leverage common application flaws. The following list provides some areas of concern:

- **Authentication flaws:**

  - **Improper login failure messages**: When a user enters either a wrong username or password, applications often reveal what the user entered incorrectly. This reveals lot of potential information from an attacker's perspective. An attacker may write an automated script to make a list of all valid users of that particular application. This can be a big risk, especially in the case of telecom and banking applications.

  - **Weak password policy**: Weak password policy is a common problem among most applications. Applications tend to allow easy, simple passwords that do not expire. The Internet has a huge collection of the most commonly used passwords which could be effectively used by attackers to bypass weak credentials.

  - **Improper password recovery mechanisms**: All applications offer mechanisms to recover a password in case the user forgets his credentials. If the password recovery mechanism isn't implemented securely, attackers can use simple techniques to evade the recovery mechanism and get the victim's credentials.

  - **Credentials transmitted over insecure communication channel**: *Sniffing* is one of the techniques widely used to intercept data traveling over the network. If the data is in plain text, the attacker can easily get access to it. If applications transfer sensitive information like user credentials over insecure HTTP, it gives rise to risk of credential compromise.

  - **Broken authentication**: An application might be using a secured communication channel and a strong password policy. But if the application doesn't check for authentication when the user tries to access sensitive parts of the application, then any unauthorized user could exploit this flaw to get into the system.

- **Authorization flaws:**

  - **Insecure direct object references**: Applications use *objects* to identify and segregate user information. A common example is usernames and their associated IDs. While two users might have the same name, the application internally assigns them unique IDs to distinguish between them. In Table 10-1, each user has been assigned a user ID. When the application needs to display a profile for user Joe, the URL would be `https://example.com/user/profile.php?id=1`.

Now Joe might be an attacker with malicious intent and simply change the URL to `https://example.com/user/profile.php?id=2` and access the profile for user Mic. This flaw is known as an *insecure direct object reference*.

Table 10-1. *Database Table with User ID and Respective Usernames*

ID	Username
1	Joe
2	Mic
3	Shon
4	Tom

- **Vertical and horizontal privilege escalation**: Privilege escalation happens whenever a user tries to get access to an area of an application she is not authorized to access. As shown in Figure 10-1, if User 1 is able to bypass access control and access resources meant for the admin user, it is known as *vertical privilege escalation*. If User 1 is able to bypass access control and access resources meant for User 2, it is known as *horizontal privilege escalation*.

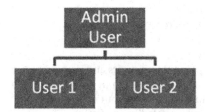

Figure 10-1. *User representation in the role hierarchy*

- **Function-level access control issues**: If the programmer or developer doesn't follow secure coding practices, it may cause function-level access control issues. To understand this, let's consider the following example:

  - A normal user visits the following URL to get information about his account: `https://example.com/users/get-account-info.php`.

  - Now the same user tries to access the URL `https://example.com/users/get-admin-account-info.php`, and gets all the information of the admin account in an unauthorized way.

  - This happened because before calling the function `get-admin-account-info`, the application didn't check whether the user is authorized to access information served by that function.

- **Session management flaws:**

  - **Weak session IDs**: A *session ID* is something that an application uses to uniquely store and process all the information for a particular user for a particular time period. If the application uses weak and simple session IDs, an attacker can easily guess or brute-force those IDs to get unauthorized access to the target application.

- **Session ID reuse**: If an application uses the same session ID before and after login, it can result in attacks like *session fixation*. Hence an application must generate a new session ID before login and after login, and it must invalidate the same session ID upon session termination.

- **Missing idle session timeout**: If the application keeps an unused session alive and active for an infinite time, this might be exploited by attackers who have access to user systems in public areas.

- **Session validity**: Some poorly coded applications tend to keep the session valid and active even if the user logs out or the browser is closed abruptly. This might be misused by an attacker to get unauthorized access.

- **Cross-site request forgery (CSRF)**: A cross-site request forgery attack is a severe potential security vulnerability in most applications that is caused by poor session management practices. To understand the CSRF attack, consider the following scenario:

  - A victim opens and logs in into a bank application in one of the tabs of the browser and her personal email in another tab.

  - An attacker sends a specially crafted URL as a link in an email to the victim.

  - The victim clicks the link sent by the attacker.

  - As soon as the victim clicks the link, funds are transferred from the victim's account to the attacker's account silently in background.

- **Input validation flaws:**

  - **Insufficient input sanitization**: All applications accept input from users and other services through forms, files, and other means. Often all of this input is trusted, accepted, and processed as-is without any sanitization. The input may contain garbage data, invalid data, or potentially dangerous data like JavaScript and SQL queries.

  - **Injection flaws**: Injection flaws are the result of lack of input validation. The end result depends on what the attacker injects as an input to the application. The most common type of injection is SQL injection, where a SQL query is injected as part of an input parameter. Instead of treating this as text, the application processes it by sending and executing the query at the back-end database. Other types of injection include LDAP injection and OS command injection.

  - Sample SQL injection queries:

    - `' or '1'='1`

    - `or 1=1 --`

    - `admin' --`

    - `select @@version`

    - `waitfor delay '0:0:20'`

  - **Cross-site scripting (XSS)**: Cross-site scripting is a very common vulnerability in web applications, wherein the attacker injects JavaScript in one of the input parameters, which is executed on the client side of the affected users. The following are the most common variants of cross-site scripting:

- **Reflected cross-site scripting**: In this type of attack, the malicious script is not stored in the vulnerable application. The attack is executed only if the victim opens and triggers a specially crafted malicious URL.

- **Stored/persistent cross site scripting**: In this type of attack, the malicious script is permanently stored in the vulnerable application, and all users of that application are affected whether or not they explicitly invoke the URL. Public forums that allow users to comment are most likely to be vulnerable to stored cross site scripting.

  Figure 10-2 shows an example of reflected cross site scripting wherein JavaScript code to alert a message box has been injected in the search field of the application.

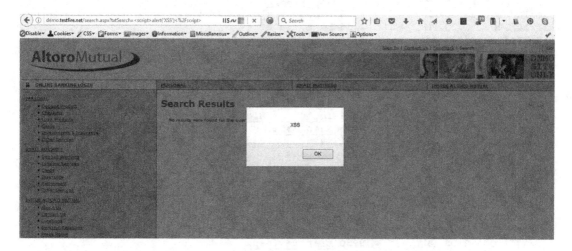

Figure 10-2. *Reflected cross site scripting vulnerability in a demo website*

- **Malicious file uploads**: Many applications offer the facility of file uploads, but they fail to check the uploaded files for malicious content. Using minor tweaks in a file extension and using special encoders, an attacker can craft an innocent-looking file, upload it to the target application, and then execute it to exploit the vulnerable system.

- **Other flaws:**

  - **Configuration management flaws**: However well-secured an application might be, if it is deployed in an insecure environment, then it is still vulnerable. *Configuration management flaws* refer to misconfigured web servers and the surrounding environment. Administrators often forget to remove old and backup files before making an application live. The admin interfaces may also be kept open to all end users instead of just the limited group. Directory listings are another such problem, which allows end users to browse through all files and directories through a web browser. Figure 10-3 shows a directory listing vulnerability.

demo.testfire.net - /bank/

```
[To Parent Directory]

  5/10/2015   4:25 AM      <dir> 20060308 bak
11/20/2006  10:05 AM       1831 account.aspx
  6/18/2015   7:41 PM       5067 account.aspx.cs
11/20/2006  10:05 AM        771 apply.aspx
11/20/2006  10:05 AM       2828 apply.aspx.cs
11/10/2006   1:20 PM       2236 bank.master
  7/16/2007   8:35 AM       1134 bank.master.cs
11/20/2006  10:05 AM        904 customize.aspx
11/20/2006  10:05 AM       1955 customize.aspx.cs
  7/23/2007   4:26 PM       1806 login.aspx
  7/23/2007   4:27 PM       5847 login.aspx.cs
11/1/2006    8:42 PM         78 logout.aspx
  7/16/2007   9:39 AM       3254 logout.aspx.cs
  7/16/2007   8:21 AM        935 main.aspx
  7/16/2007   9:36 AM       3951 main.aspx.cs
  5/10/2015   4:25 AM      <dir> members
  1/12/2007   1:55 PM       1414 mozxpath.js
11/20/2006  10:05 AM        785 queryxpath.aspx
11/20/2006  10:05 AM       1838 queryxpath.aspx.cs
  7/18/2007   5:13 PM        499 servererror.aspx
  7/18/2007   4:13 PM       1700 transaction.aspx
  6/18/2015   7:41 PM       3867 transaction.aspx.cs
  7/17/2007   3:03 PM       3930 transfer.aspx
  6/18/2015   7:41 PM       3505 transfer.aspx.cs
  7/17/2007   2:44 PM         82 ws.asmx
```

Figure 10-3. *Directory listing vulnerability in a demo website*

- **Cryptography flaws**: Cryptography is primarily used to provide confidentiality. However, if a weak cryptographic algorithm is used to encrypt the data, it can be easily cracked to get access to the original plain text. The cryptographic keys are also often not kept secured. Once the attacker gains access to the cryptographic keys, she can easily decrypt the cipher text and compromise its confidentiality.

- **Using components with known vulnerabilities**: Many developers have a habit of using third-party components while developing new applications. These third-party components might themselves be vulnerable to various security risks, however. If such vulnerable components are used, then the new application inherently becomes vulnerable.

- **Business logic flaws**: Every application contains some business logic, which provides the core rules for how the application should function. It's quite possible that the business logic itself isn't foolproof and has some flaws. Such flaws can be exploited by attackers to compromise the application. They can only be revealed upon careful review of the application architecture and design. Automated scanning tools aren't intelligent enough to catch business logic flaws. For example, an application may pass some value to an external application; however, it might not verify whether the same value is being returned. An attacker can tamper with the transaction and modify values in response. In this case the integrity of the transaction is being compromised.

Web Application Hacking Methodology

Web application hacking is not just about using automated tools to find common vulnerabilities. It is indeed a methodological approach that, if followed, would help reveal many more flaws and potential security vulnerabilities. The following section describes the systematic approach and process to be followed for testing the security of web applications.

- **Analyzing web applications**: The first step is to understand and analyze the target application. Unless and until sufficient details about the target application are known, one cannot proceed with further testing. Some of the information that needs to be gathered is:

  - What is the purpose of the target application?

  - Who is the audience of the target application?

  - How critical is the application from a business perspective?

  - What technology platform has been used to develop the application?

  - What are the important workflows in the target application?

- **Identifying the entry and exit points**: The next step is to identify entry and exit points. This gives an idea of how an attacker might try to intrude into the application. The entry point may be a login screen or a registration form.

- **Breaking down the components**: This step involves breaking down application components. It's vital to know what components are used within the application, whether it involves an additional application server and/or database server, and similar questions.

- **Testing manually for vulnerabilities**: Using tools like BurpSuite, Paros, ZAP, and others, manual security testing can be performed. This mainly involves intercepting potential HTTP requests, modifying and tampering with the parameter values, and then analyzing the application's response.

- **Automated security scanning**: Tools like IBM AppScan, Fortify, and Accunetix are some of the commercial tools available for automated web application security testing. They perform a comprehensive scan on input parameters across the application and check for various vulnerabilities.

- **Removing false positives**: Automated scanning tools may produce false positives. Hence it is important to manually verify any vulnerability found during scanning and remove false positives if any.

- **Reporting with remediation**: A certain security issue might appear as merely a missing functionality to a developer. Hence, it is critical to prepare a vulnerability report with all necessary artifacts and proof-of-concepts in order to make the developer community understand the severity of the vulnerabilities identified. It is also necessary to suggest a fix recommendation for any identified vulnerability.

Hacking Web Servers

Once the attacker has footprinted information about a web server, he can then use various vulnerability scanners to explore more vulnerabilities in order to compromise the server. If a web server is not configured securely, it leaves open potential security vulnerabilities. Nikto is one such open source tool which scans for potentially dangerous files and programs and checks for outdated server versions and other version-specific problems of various servers (Figure 10-4).

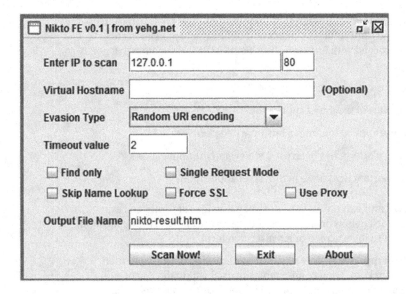

Figure 10-4. *Nikto GUI for scanning web server vulnerabilities*

Automated Scanning Tools

While it is possible to test web applications manually for various security vulnerabilities like SQL injection, cross-site scripting, and so on, there are many tools available that automate the web application security testing process. Some tools, like IBM AppScan, HP Fortify, and BurpSuite Pro are commercially available, while others, like OWASP ZAP, Arachni, and Paros are open source and free alternatives for performing security scanning on web applications.

Following are the advantages of using automated web application security testing tools:

- In any given application, there are tons of input parameters, some of which are directly visible while others are hidden. It's not possible to test all parameters manually. Automated scanning tools try to improve scan coverage significantly, making it possible to detect more vulnerabilities.

- Automated scanning tools have multiple variants of attack vectors predefined; hence they have a better chance of detecting vulnerabilities.

Following are the disadvantages of using automated web application security testing tools:

- Many of the tools produce numerous false positives.

- An automated scanning tool usually generates a large number of traffic requests. It may raise an alarm, and the request might be blocked by a firewall.

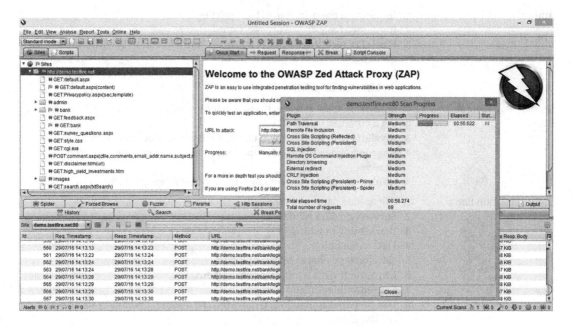

Figure 10-5. *The OWAS ZAP tool, used for automated security testing*

Mitigations

So far in this chapter, we have seen various web application vulnerabilities and ways to exploit them. However it is equally important to know about the possible controls to prevent or mitigate these vulnerabilities. Table 10-2 lists common web application flaws along with their mitigations.

Table 10-2. *Mitigations for Common Web Application Flaws*

Flaw	Mitigation in Brief
Authentication flaws	1. Set a strong password policy. 2. Implement password salting. 3. Implement password masking (****). 4. Display generic and standard messages in case of authentication failure. 5. Validate password policy at both the client side and server side. 6. Encrypt the password in storage using a strong algorithm. 7. Implement a secure password recovery mechanism. 8. Use multifactor authentication for sensitive areas. 9. Verify the old password while changing to a new password. 10. Make use of OAuth, OpenID, and Kerberos or similar tools for implementing single sign-on (SSO).
Authorization flaws	1. Implement the principle of least privilege. 2. Implement role-based access control. 3. Use JSON web tokens (JWT) for secure authentication and information exchange. 4. Implement validation checks to prevent authorization creep, and vertical and horizontal privilege escalation.
Session management flaws	1. Set an idle session timeout value to limit the duration. 2. Set a complex session ID. 3. Invalidate the session upon termination of the browser window. 4. Regenerate new session ID upon successful authentication or privilege change. 5. Implement protection for cross-site request forgery (CSRF).
Input validation flaws	1. Client-side data validation. 2. Server-side data validation. 3. Blacklisting or whitelisting of input characters. 4. Data sanitization. 5. Content type checks for file uploads. 6. Implement virus scanner for file uploads. 7. Output validation and encoding. 8. Use prepared statements, parameterized queries, and bind variables in the database.
Auditing and logging flaws	1. Capture login/logout, failed login, new user creation, and data modification events. Password changes and detailed activity events should also be captured along with user name, timestamp, and the end user's source IP address. 2. Ensure that logging cannot be used to deplete system resources, for example by filling up disk space or exceeding the database transaction log space, leading to denial of service. 3. Ensure that logs are protected from tampering.

Summary

- An *attack vector* is a path through which an attacker gains unauthorized access to the target system.

- *Privilege escalation* happens whenever a user tries to get access to the area of an application that he or she is not authorized to access.

- A session ID is something an application uses to uniquely store and process all the information for a particular user for a particular time period.

- From a security perspective it is important that an application generates a new random and complex session ID after login and destroys it after session termination.

- Lack of input validation leads to problems like SQL injection, cross-site scripting, and others.

- The environment in which the application is deployed must also be secured.

Do-It-Yourself Exercises

- Download and install OWASP Web Goat and try to solve the web application hacking challenges.

- Download, install, and explore the OWASP ZAP tool.

Test Your Knowledge: Sample Questions

1. Which of the following is a small piece of information that is sent from a website to the client system and is retained for further tracking?

    a. HTTP

    b. Cookie

    c. XML

    d. None of the above

2. It is safe to use the same session ID before and after login. True or False?

    a. True

    b. False

3. Which of the following attacks store a script permanently into the vulnerable application?

    a. Reflected cross-site scripting

    b. SQL injection

    c. Persistent cross-site scripting

    d. None of the above

4. Which of the following would help prevent SQL injection?

    a. Using HTTPS

    b. Installing anti-virus software

    c. Using a parameterized query

    d. All of the above

CHAPTER 11

■ ■ ■

Wireless Hacking

The popularity of wireless networks is rapidly increasing thanks to its ease of use and convenience. However, like any other technology, wireless networks also come with some inherent security risks. This chapter covers the basics of wireless networks like Bluetooth and Wi-Fi, along with their common threats.

■ **Key Topics**   Introduction to wireless networking, types of wireless networks, wireless standards, common Wi-Fi terms, Wi-Fi authentication, wireless encryption, wireless hacking methodology, Wi-Fi security best practices, Bluetooth hacking, defending against Bluetooth attacks.

Wireless Networking Primer

As the name suggests, a wireless network is a way of connecting systems without the use of cables. Any medium- or large-scaled organization has hundreds and thousands of systems connected in a network. This involves extensive cabling. In the case of a network problem, it can be tedious to trace back the exact cable that caused the fault. With the introduction of wireless networks, end user connectivity, scalability, and troubleshooting are greatly simplified.

The following are some advantages of a wireless network:

- **Convenience**: In a conventional wired network, as the size of the network grows, the cabling also grows significantly. Cabling not only adds to cost but also consumes space. With a wireless network, it is easy to expand the network without adding complexity of cables.

- **Mobility**: In a wired network, a user has to be at a fixed place in order to access the network. With the use of a wireless network, users can simply roam in the premises and still access the network resources.

- **Ease of deployment**: A wireless network simply needs an access point in order to get started. A new wireless network can be configured and brought up in very little time.

- **Scalability**: In a wireless network, new users can be added easily without additional cost as compared to a wired network, where adding a new user would require additional cabling.

- **Reduced cost**: Because there is no cabling involved, setting up a wireless network is much cheaper than setting up a wired network.

The following are some disadvantages of a wireless network:

- **Security**: Security is one of the major concerns in Wi-Fi networks. Open networks (without authentication) can be accessed and misused by anyone in the vicinity. There is also a possibility of intercepting traffic if not encrypted.

- **Reliability**: Because Wi-Fi works over radio frequency, it is subject to interference. Any obstacles, such as walls, significantly decrease the range and speed of the network.

The following are the various types of wireless networks:

- **Extension to wired network**: Many times it happens that an organization has a fixed wired network. But there might be visitors and guests coming into the organization premises who need limited network access. For security reasons it might not be advisable to give wired access to the network for such visitors and guests. Hence, an extension to existing wired connection using Wi-Fi becomes a feasible solution. All visiting guests can easily connect to this extended Wi-Fi network, which has limited, restricted, and regulated access to the network.

- **Multiple access points**: An organization might have widespread premises, and so to ensure that all users in the premises have stable connectivity to the wireless network, multiple access points are installed at various places. Each access point serves users within its range.

- **LAN-LAN wireless connection**: Suppose an organization has offices in two adjacent buildings separated by some distance apart. The office in each of the building has wired LAN connectivity. Because of some operational challenges, it's not possible to lay cable between the two buildings. Hence, to connect the wired LANs in the two buildings, a wireless network could be used. Using an access point, wired networks in both buildings could be easily bridged.

- **3G/4G hotspots**: 3G/4G hotspots have currently become very common in the form of data cards and dongles. These devices accommodate a 3G/4G SIM card for Internet connectivity and share the Internet with multiple devices over Wi-Fi. These devices are extremely lightweight and portable, and so they are very popular among people on the move.

Wireless Standards

The technical specification for the functioning of a wireless network is specified in standard IEEE 802.11. The base standard 802.11 is further specified based on various amendments. The classification is mainly based on the speed, range, and reliability that each standard offers. Some of the common subtype standards are listed in Table 11-1.

Table 11-1. *Wireless Standards with Their Features*

Standard	Speed	Other Features
802.11 a	Up to 54 MB/Sec	Expensive but less prone to interference.
802.11 b	Up to 11 MB/Sec	Prone to interference but less expensive.
802.11 g	Up to 54 MB/Sec	Better signal strength compared to 802.11b but more costly.
802.11 n	Up to 700 MB/Sec	Better performance, range, and improved reliability.

Common Wi-Fi terminology includes the following terms:

- **Hotspot**: A *hotspot* is any physical area where people can access the Internet through a wireless network. Hotspots are very common at restaurants, hotels, coffee shops, airports, parks, libraries, and other public places.

- **Access point**: An *access point* is a hardware device that is used to create a wireless network. It can be used to connect different systems on the same network or interconnect between a LAN and a WLAN. Depending on the antenna used by the access point, it has a range within which users can connect to it. Access points are often used to extend the existing wired LAN to other systems and users for enhanced mobility.

- **BSSID (Basic Service Set Identifier)**: The MAC address or the physical address of the access point (similar to the MAC address of an Ethernet card). It is a unique identifier assigned by the manufacturer of the access point.

- **Bandwidth**: *Bandwidth* is the amount of data that can be transferred from one system to another in a unit of time. It is often measured in units like MB/sec, GB/sec, and TB/sec. The bandwidth of the wireless network depends on the capability of the access point.

SSID

In simple terms, the *Service Set Identifier (SSID)* is the name by which a wireless network is identified. When you purchase a new wireless router and configure it for the first time, it will have a default SSID (usually the name of the manufacturer, such as Linksys). You can then change it to any name of your choice (up to 32 characters). Once that is done, whenever anyone in range of your wireless network searches for available wireless connections (on PC, mobile, and so on), the SSID will appear in the list (provided SSID broadcasting hasn't been turned off). If you decide to turn off the SSID broadcast, then no one will be able to search your wireless network and connect to it unless they manually enter the SSID name. This is often done to restrict the use of the wireless network to limited people.

Wi-Fi Authentication

An open wireless connection with no user authentication can attract many unwanted guests and unauthorized users. In order to restrict the use of wireless network to legitimate users, it is necessary to implement an authentication mechanism for all users connecting to the wireless network. Following are some of the types of wireless authentication:

- **Open System Authentication (OSA):** The default authentication protocol for the IEEE 802.11 standard. The process of this authentication is completed in three steps:

  1. The computer that wants the wireless network access sends an authentication request to the access point.

  2. The access point in response generates a random authentication code, which is valid only for that particular session.

  3. The computer that requested the access accepts the code and is connected to the network.

- **Shared-Key authentication.** The process of this authentication is completed in five steps:

  1. The computer that wants wireless network access sends an authentication request to the access point.

  2. The access point in response generates a challenge text and sends it back to the computer.

  3. The computer then encrypts the challenge text with the WEP key and sends the message to the access point.

  4. The access point decrypts the message and compares it to the original challenge text. If the two texts are exactly the same, then the access point sends the final authentication code to the computer.

  5. The computer accepts the authentication code from the access point and is connected to the network.

- **Wi-Fi authentication using centralized server:** Besides the previous techniques, a computer requesting access to a wireless network can also be authenticated using a centralized authentication server like Active Directory, LDAP (Light Weight Directory Access Protocol), or RADIUS.

Searching for Wi-Fi Networks

The use of wireless networks has increased exponentially over the last decade or so. Wi-Fi is being extensively used not only by corporate organizations but also by individuals and home users. If you walk or drive through your city you may find tons of wireless networks. It can be quite interesting to do a survey of wireless networks in your vicinity and filter open connections without any authentication. Following are some of the techniques used for this purpose:

- **Wardriving:** Wardriving is a technique in which a person with a Wi-Fi–enabled laptop or mobile drives through the city scanning for Wi-Fi networks. Using GPS, the person can then generate a map of areas with active wireless networks. The results can be filtered based on locality, authentication type, signal strength, and so on. There are many free tools available to aid with this activity.

- **Warchalking:** Warchalking is quite similar to Wardriving. However in Warchalking, when a person finds an open Wi-Fi network providing Internet access, he marks that place with a special symbol using a chalk. This is an indication to others passing through the area that an interconnection is available for use over Wi-Fi.

Table 11-2 lists the different types of wireless encryption.

Table 11-2. *Comparison between Various Wireless Encryption Standards*

	WEP	WPA	WPA2
Full Form	Wired Equivalent Privacy	Wi-Fi Protected Access	Wi-Fi Protected Access V2
Encryption	RC4 with 40-bit keys	TKIP with 128-bit key and constant key rotation	AES-CCMP and constant key rotation
Authentication	Pre-shared keys	802.1x with EAP and RADIUS	802.1x with EAP and RADIUS
Key Management	Manual key rotation	Per-packet key rotation	Per-packet key rotation and per-session key rotation

Common Wireless Threats

1. **Wi-Fi signal jamming**: Jamming involves the blocking of all communications completely. It is done with help of special hardware. Once the attacker uses a jamming device, all the wireless networks within its vicinity are blocked. Users are not able to connect to the wireless network any more.

2. **Misconfigured access point attack**: Many organizations or individual users buy access points and use them with default settings. They don't bother to configure the access point securely. Attackers can easily exploit such weakly configured access points to get unauthorized entry into the network.

3. **Rogue access point attack**: A rogue access point is a specially crafted fake access point that makes user believe it is genuine. When the user innocently connects to the rogue access point, the attacker sniffs all the sensitive information from the session.

4. **Eavesdropping**: Eavesdropping is a way of capturing and decoding all clear-text traffic to obtain sensitive information.

Wireless Hacking Methodology

The wireless hacking methodology consists of the following basic steps:

1. **Discovering Wi-Fi networks**: This is the first step in making an attempt to compromise a Wi-Fi network. In this step, various Wi-Fi discovery tools (like NetStumbler, NetSurveyor, and so on) are used to scan the available networks within range.

2. **GPS mapping**: Once a list of Wi-Fi networks is obtained, it can then be geographically visualized using maps. WiGLE is one such web-based service, which accepts feeds from Wi-Fi scanners and shows the listed networks on maps.

3. **Wireless traffic analysis:** This step involves setting up the correct hardware and software for Wi-Fi hacking. Some operating systems, like Windows, allow you to listen to traffic but don't permit you to inject Wi-Fi traffic, while others, like Linux, allow both. Also, some important tools used in Wi-Fi hacking like Aircrack-ng work only with specific Wireless adapters. Once the right hardware and software has been set up, tools like Wireshark can be used to analyze wireless traffic.

4. **Execute attacks**: Once the initial reconnaissance has been done, it's time to execute attacks on the target wireless network.

   a. **Fragmentation attack**: By launching a successful fragmentation attack, we can obtain up to 1500 bytes of PRGA (Pseudo Random Generation Algorithm). This attack doesn't reveal the WEP key but just fetches the PRGA. Once the PRGA is obtained, it can be used to generate packets that are then used for various wireless injection attacks.

   b. **MAC-spoofing**: Many access points have MAC filtering enabled. This means only those devices whose MAC ID is in the access point's whitelist can connect to the wireless network. To bypass this, MAC address spoofing can be used to change the MAC address of a wireless adapter to the one matching the access point's MAC whitelist. SMAC is one such tool on Windows that helps change the MAC address of network adapters.

   c. **De-authentication attack**: This type of attack is used to forcefully disconnect users who are actively connected on the target access point. This is a type of denial-of-service attack.

   d. **Man-in-the-middle attack**: In this type of attack the attacker first de-authorizes a valid active user from the access point then forces the victim user to connect to a fake access point, and finally intercepts all the data that the victim sends and receives during the session.

   e. **Evil twin attack**: In this type of attack the attacker sets up an access point that pretends to be legitimate by imitating another genuine access point within the area. Users connect to the rogue access point, which is exactly the twin of the original access point. Once the users are associated with the rogue access point, the attacker can then intercept and tamper all network traffic passing through it.

5. **Break Wi-Fi encryption**: The next step involves finding the encryption key used in the target wireless network. The Aircrack toolset, which includes tools like `airmon-ng`, `airodump-ng`, `airreplay-ng` and `aircrack-ng`, can be effectively used to crack the encryption key.

Spectrum Analysis

Spectrum analysis is a way of examining Wi-Fi radio transmissions to obtain useful and valuable information. This involves measuring the power of radio signals and then converting it into binary sequences. RF spectrum analyzers are mainly used by RF technicians to install and troubleshoot wireless networks. Spectrum analysis effectively helps detect interference in the wireless networks.

Following are some common Wi-Fi security best practices:

- **Changing the defaults**: When a new Access Point is purchased fresh from market, it comes with default credentials and configuration. This needs to be changed before use.

- **Turning off SSID broadcasts**: If all the users of the network know the existence of the network, there may not be a need to broadcast and advertise SSID to unwanted users.

- **Using strong encryption**: Using WPA2 or WPA2 Enterprise considerably reduces the risk of the wireless network being compromised.

- **Enabling MAC filtering**: This setting allows access to only those devices whose MAC addresses are in the whitelist of the access point.

- **Upgrading the access point software**: On a regular basis, it is important to check whether there are any updates available for the firmware of the access point. If the access point firmware is kept outdated, it might have inherent vulnerabilities that could be exploited.

Bluetooth Hacking

Bluetooth provides various modes depending on whether the device is to be made visible to others. Following are some of the modes in which Bluetooth can operate:

- **Discoverable**: When a Bluetooth device is set to Discoverable mode, it becomes permanently visible to all other devices that are searching for Bluetooth connections.

- **Limited discoverable**: In this mode, the device is made visible to other devices only for a limited duration (for example, 30 seconds). After the duration is over, it becomes invisible to all other devices.

- **Nondiscoverable**: This mode sets the device to invisible mode. No other device can search a device that is set in Nondiscoverable mode.

Bluetooth Pairing

Bluetooth pairing is one of the steps involved when two Bluetooth devices connect with each other for the first time. This involves PIN authentication. Once the devices are paired successfully, they can then communicate with each other and transfer data.

Common Bluetooth Threats

Although Bluetooth is extremely convenient for short-range wireless data transfers, it also has several security risks if not configured and used securely. Following are some of the common Bluetooth threats:

- **Loss of personal data**: An attacker can exploit existing Bluetooth vulnerabilities to steal personal and confidential data like contacts, SMS (Short Message Service text messages), call logs, and so on over Bluetooth and use it for malicious purposes.

- **Hijacking**: An attacker could completely hijack a device over Bluetooth and act without the user's interaction. This includes making calls, recording ongoing conversations, and the like.

- **Sending SMS**: An attacker can make use of the compromised Bluetooth device to send SMS to any person to hide his own identity. This is mainly done for terrorist activities.

- **Using airtime**: An attacker could make international calls from a device compromised over Bluetooth and cause severe financial damage to victim.

- **Malicious code**: An attacker can send malware over Bluetooth that would infect the device permanently and modify, steal, or destroy sensitive user data on the device.

- **Inherent vulnerabilities**: The Bluetooth stack as a whole may have some inherent vulnerabilities that might be exploited.

- **Bluejacking**: *Bluejacking* is a process of forcefully sending unwanted messages to the victim over Bluetooth. It is similar to email spamming. Though it is not very harmful, it can cause nuisance to the victim. It is often used for forceful marketing.

- **Bluesniff**: Bluesniff is a utility on Linux that is used for Bluetooth wardriving. It is useful for finding hidden and discoverable Bluetooth devices.

- **Bluesmacking**: *Bluesmacking* is a type of Denial of Service attack over Bluetooth. In this attack, an oversized packet is sent to a victim's device over Bluetooth, which causes it to crash.

- **Bluesnarfing**: *Bluesnarfing* makes use of a vulnerability in the Bluetooth stack to gain unauthorized access to sensitive information on the victim's device. The attacker can gain access to the victim's phonebook and calendar entries through this attack.

Defending against Bluetooth Attacks

In the previous section, we saw various attacks over Bluetooth. However with some simple precautions, it's possible to prevent these attacks. Following are some of the ways to prevent Bluetooth attacks.

- **Changing default PINs**: PINs are required for pairing Bluetooth devices. Many devices tend to use default and easy PINs for pairing. Such default PINs should be changed to custom complex PIN.

- **Hidden mode**: The device should be kept in nondiscoverable mode when not intended to pair with any new device.

- **Monitoring paired devices**: A list of previously paired devices should be reviewed frequently, and all unwanted or unknown devices should be deleted immediately.

- **Enabling Bluetooth only when needed**: Bluetooth should be enabled only when required and should be turned off at all other times.

- **Reviewing pairing requests**: Any new pairing request should be reviewed for its genuineness and should not be blindly accepted. A pairing request from any unknown device source should be rejected.

Summary

Following are the key topics discussed in the chapter:

- Wireless networking is a way of connecting systems without the use of cables.

- The technical specification for functioning of a wireless network is defined in standard IEEE 802.11.

- A *hotspot* is any physical area where use of Internet is available through a wireless network.

- An *access point* is a hardware device that is used to create a wireless network.

- BSSID stands for Basic Service Set Identifier. It is the MAC address or the physical address of the access point.

- SSID stands for Service Set Identifier. In simple terms, it is the name by which a wireless network is identified.

- *Wardriving* is a technique wherein a person with a Wi-Fi–enabled laptop or mobile drives through a city scanning for Wi-Fi networks.

- Wired Equivalent Privacy (WEP), Wi-Fi Protected Access (WPA), and Wi-Fi Protected Access Version 2 (WPA2) are commonly used types of wireless encryption.

- *Bluejacking, bluesniffing, bluesmacking,* and *bluesnarfing* are common attacks on Bluetooth devices.

Do-It-Yourself (DIY) Exercises

1. Harden any Wi-Fi access point according to wireless security best practices.

2. Perform wardriving in your locality and generate a map out of the result.

Test Your Knowledge: Sample Questions

1. The SSID is the MAC address of the access point. True or False?

   a. True

   b. False

2. Which of the following is not a subtype of 802.11 network?

   a. 802.11b

   b. 802.11ay

   c. 802.11g

   d. 802.11n

3. Which of the following is a technique for examining Wi-Fi radio transmissions to obtain useful and valuable information?

   a. Radio analysis

   b. Spectrum analysis

   c. Bandwidth monitoring

   d. None of the above

CHAPTER 12

Hacking Mobile Platforms

The rise in the use of mobile devices and smartphones has also increased the risk of compromise of sensitive personal data present on these devices. This chapter introduces the two most popular mobile platforms, Android and iOS, along with their security implications.

■ **Key Topics**   Mobile terminology, mobile attack vectors, overview of Android OS, components of an Android application, Android application security testing, iOS jailbreaking, iOS security guidelines, mobile device management.

Mobile Terminology

Following are some terms you should know in order to get the most out of mobile security:

- **Stock ROM**: The operating system of a mobile device is stored in ROM, and *stock ROM* is nothing but the default ROM—that is, the operating system—provided by the device manufacturer. Manufacturers usually also provide a customized version of the ROM with some added features.

- **Custom ROM**: *Custom ROM* is a ROM developed and built by a third-party vendor. The vendor builds custom ROMs for devices of various manufacturers. A custom ROM offers more fine-grained user controls and flexibility than the stock ROM. However, replacing the stock ROM with a custom ROM may void the warranty of the device.

- **Device brick**: *Device bricking* is a state of the device from which it cannot be recovered back to normal. Bricking the device makes it permanently unusable. Playing around with the device firmware may cause the device to brick.

- **BYOD**: *Bring Your Own Device* is a type of organizational policy that permits employees to bring in and use their personal mobile devices for official work.

Common Mobile Attack Vectors

With an exponential rise in the use of mobile technology, almost all businesses are going mobile. However, the mobile ecosystem isn't yet secured enough to address various threats. Mobile applications and the mobile operating systems are often compromised by attackers to get unauthorized access to sensitive data on personal devices. Following are some of the attack vectors commonly used to compromise mobile systems:

© Sagar Ajay Rahalkar 2016
S.A. Rahalkar, *Certified Ethical Hacker (CEH) Foundation Guide*, DOI 10.1007/978-1-4842-2325-3_12

- **Malware:** With the rapidly increasing use of mobile devices, malware applications are now targeting mobile devices with the intent to steal personal data stored on the device memory.

- **Application/OS modification:** While the stock ROM has restrictive permissions, the custom or modified ROM comes from a third-party vendor with no trust. It's quite possible that such custom ROM contains some back door, allowing remote entry to the attacker.

- **Jail-broken device:** *Jailbreaking* a device loosens the overall security and permission model of the system. It allows installing unknown and untrusted apps, which may leave the device vulnerable to various attacks.

- **Application vulnerabilities:** Almost all mobile applications are developed keeping only business requirements in mind, and security is often ignored. All the vulnerabilities that apply to normal web applications, like injection attacks, XSS, insecure data storage, and so on, also apply to mobile applications. A vulnerable mobile application may leak the user's personal data as well as open up a path to compromise other applications on the same device.

- **Loss of device:** Accidental loss or theft of devices has also become a common problem. The stolen device may contain confidential, sensitive, and private data which could be misused against the victim.

Overview of Android OS

Android is a Linux-based operating system designed to operate on portable devices like PDAs, smartphones, tablet PCs, smart watches, and the like. Following are some components of the Android system:

- **Linux kernel:** This is the core of the Android system. It consists of low-level device drivers, memory and power management components, and other basic elements.

- **Android Runtime:** This includes some libraries and the Dalvik virtual machine. The libraries allow the developers to develop Android applications using Java, and the Dalvik virtual machine is used for executing Android applications.

- **Libraries:** Libraries contain the actual pieces of code that provide various features on the Android OS. The Android core library includes SQLite, OpenGL, SSL, and similar tools.

- **Applications:** Some applications are provided by default on the Android OS, including SMS, Calendar, and Contacts, while users can also install custom third-party applications from other trusted sources.

Components of Android Application

From an end-user perspective, an Android application may appear as a simple standalone application. However, any Android application consists of many components that work in the background to accomplish the given task. Following are some of the components of an Android application.

- **Activities:** An Android *activity* represents any single screen on the user interface. For example, a simple login screen with username and password is one activity of the application. Applications invoke activities based on the workflow.

- **Services**: An Android *service* is a component that runs silently in the background to perform certain operations. For example, a service may fetch some remote data while the user is busy reading the content on a particular page of an application.

- **Broadcast receivers**: Android applications continuously broadcast messages so that other applications know about the event and could possibly trigger some action. *Broadcast receivers* are used to respond to broadcast messages sent by other applications or by the Android system.

- **Content Providers**: Content providers do the job of supplying data to other applications based on specific requests. Content providers are one of the best ways for cross-application data sharing.

- **Manifest**: This is an XML file that contains all configuration parameters of an Android application.

Android Security Testing

Similar to the web application security testing methodology, Android apps can be tested either manually or using automated tools. Let's review both manual and automated testing.

Manual Testing

Manual testing can be done by setting up an interceptor proxy (like Burp Suite, ZAP, or similar tools) on your PC and then pointing your Android device to the proxy so that all communications can be intercepted and fuzzed. Once the communication requests are intercepted, they can be easily tested for various flaws by fuzzing, or tampering with the requests. An Android application (APK) can also be decompiled to get the source code. Upon obtaining the source code, one can analyze it for possible vulnerabilities. Figure 12-1 shows apktool, which is used to decompile an APK file.

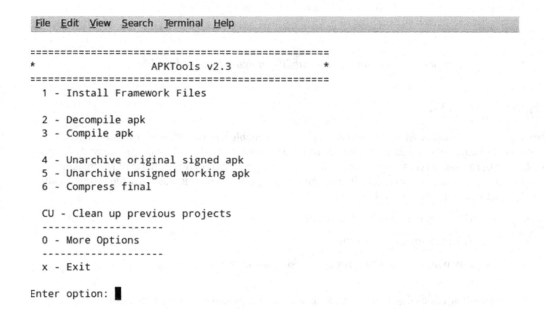

```
File  Edit  View  Search  Terminal  Help

=====================================================
*                    APKTools v2.3                   *
=====================================================
 1 - Install Framework Files

 2 - Decompile apk
 3 - Compile apk

 4 - Unarchive original signed apk
 5 - Unarchive unsigned working apk
 6 - Compress final

 CU - Clean up previous projects
 --------------------
 0 - More Options
 --------------------
 x - Exit

Enter option: █
```

Figure 12-1. *The APKTool utility for decompiling Android applications*

Automated Testing

Automated testing can be done using special-purpose testing frameworks like Drozer, an Android pen-testing framework. Using it involves setting up a Drozer agent on the Android device and then connecting to it via ADB (Android debug bridge) on a PC. Once connected, the Drozer framework can assess the attack surface area of the target application and find flaws, if any (Figure 12-2).

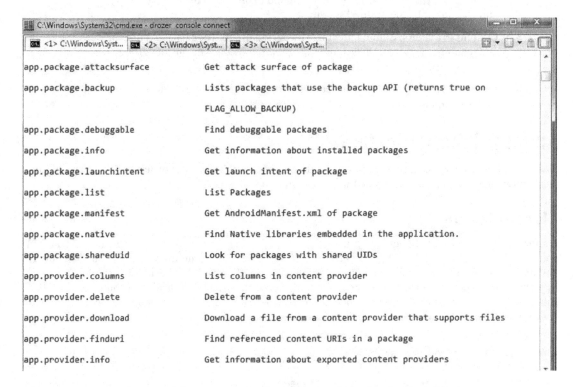

Figure 12-2. *Drozer framework for automated vulnerability analysis of Android applications*

Jaibreaking iOS

Jailbreaking is a process of applying custom kernel patches to enable the execution of all third-party applications from unknown or untrusted sources, which are unsigned by the OS vendor. Successful jailbreaking gives root-level access to the device, bypassing its permissions and restrictions. Jailbreaking also removes all the sandbox restrictions, allowing malicious applications to access restricted resources and information. Jailbreaking comes with the following risks:

- The device warranty is voided if jailbroken.

- The device performance may suffer.

- If a corrupt patch is applied during jailbreaking, the device might become unusable forever.

- Jailbreaking opens the door to installing untrusted apps and hence increases risk of malware intrusion.

Cydia is an application platform which is specifically designed for jailbroken devices. It allows users to install third-party apps and other customizations.

iOS Security Guidelines

Following are some of the guidelines and best practices for securing iOS devices:

- Lock the device with a passcode (PIN).

- Connect the iOS device only to secured wireless networks.

- Install only trusted applications from known sources on the iOS device.

- Do not jailbreak the iOS device.

- Enable jailbreak detection.

- Secure access to iTunes Apple ID.

- Disable iCloud services to prevent sensitive or confidential data from being backed up on the Cloud.

- Set up and configure Find My iPhone to locate the device if lost or stolen.

- Do not open attachments from unknown sources.

Mobile Device Management

Organizational policies like BYOD are gaining popularity but also bringing in new risks and challenges. Mobile device management (MDM) solutions allow for over-the-air or wired distribution of applications, configuration settings, patches, and updates for various types of mobile devices like smartphones, tablet PCs, and the like. A mobile device management solution helps the administrator to centrally monitor, manage, and enforce policies and restrictions on all mobile devices in scope. Without MDM, it would be difficult to monitor and manage every device traversing through the corporate network. Some of the popular MDM solutions are:

- Citrix XenMObile MDM

- IBM MaaS360

- AirWatch

- TarmacMDM

- SOTI MobiControl

Summary

Following are the key takeaways from this chapter:

- Stock ROM is the default operating system provided by the mobile manufacturer.

- Installing a custom ROM voids the device warranty and also has a risk of damaging the device.

- The Android operating system is based on the Linux kernel.

- A single user screen within an Android application is known as an *activity*.

- *Bring Your Own Device (BYOD)* is an organizational policy that allows use of personal mobile devices for official work.

- A *manifest* is an XML file that contains all configuration parameters for an Android application.

- *Jailbreaking* an iOS device removes several restrictions and enables installation of untrusted third-party applications.

- *Mobile device management* allows centralized configuration, policy enforcement, and monitoring for all mobile devices in the network.

Do-It-Yourself (DIY) Exercises

1. Download and install Visual Studio Emulator for Android and run any Android OS of your choice.

2. Download APKTool and try to decompile any Android APK.

3. Download, install and explore various options in the Drozer framework.

Test Your Knowledge: Sample Questions

1. The operating system that comes installed by default from the mobile manufacturer is known as what?

   a. Custom ROM

   b. Stock ROM

   c. Original ROM

   d. User ROM

2. The Android operating system uses the Linux kernel at its core. True or False?

   a. True

   b. False

3. Which of the following represents a single screen in an Android application?

    a. Service

    b. Broadcast

    c. Activity

    d. None of the above

4. What is Cydia?

    a. A security application on iOS

    b. An internet browser on iOS

    c. An application platform for installing third-party applications on iOS

    d. An internal system process in iOS

5. Which of the following is a framework for testing vulnerabilities in an Android application?

    a. APKTool

    b. ADB

    c. Drozer

    d. Manifest tool

CHAPTER 13

■ ■ ■

IDSes, Firewalls, and Honeypots

Routers, switches, and hubs are some of the networking devices used to establish connectivity among networked devices. However, they don't provide much control over access and security. Securing the network requires special-purpose devices like intrusion detection systems, firewalls, and honeypots. This chapter introduces these devices, their types, and the architectural considerations for their placement in the network.

■ **Key Topics** What is an IDS? How an IDS works, types of IDS, evading an IDS, symptoms of Intrusion. What is a firewall? Firewall architecture, the DMZ, types of firewalls, firewall identification techniques, evading firewalls, honeypots and their types, detecting honeypots.

What an IDS Is and How It Works

An intrusion detection system (IDS) is a system that listens to and monitors the network traffic and alerts the network administrator when any type of intrusion is detected. It checks for unusual and suspicious traffic. The IDS is essentially a packet sniffer that intercepts and analyzes all packets and searches for intrusion patterns. As soon as the IDS detects an intrusion and raises an alarm, the administrator can take appropriate action to stop or reduce the impact of intrusion.

Intrusion detection systems mainly work using signatures. They have a predefined signature database for various types of attacks. Following is a high-level overview of how an IDS works:

- For each packet that passes through the IDS, it tries to match the content against the signature database. Some IDS systems also work on behavior and anomalies.

- If the IDS finds a signature match, then it either drops the packet or blocks the source IP or notifies the administrator to take appropriate action.

Using the signature detection method, an IDS would only be able to detect those intrusions for which the signature is in its database. Anomaly detection looks for behavioral patterns. For example, there might be a system in the network that has suddenly started uploading a huge amount of traffic in the network. Such behavior might be unusual, and the IDS may detect it and further analyze it for any traces of intrusion.

Types of IDS

Based on where the IDS is placed in the network and how it functions, IDSes can be classified into various types as follows:

© Sagar Ajay Rahalkar 2016
S.A. Rahalkar, *Certified Ethical Hacker (CEH) Foundation Guide*, DOI 10.1007/978-1-4842-2325-3_13

- **Network-based IDS**: A network-based IDS intercepts, monitors, and analyzes every packet entering and leaving the network irrespective of whether that packet is permitted in the network or not. It is mainly designed to identify unusual packet behaviors at the router level. It is implemented by installing a system in promiscuous mode.

- **Host-based IDS**: The host-based IDS is aimed at identifying host-level intrusions. It is typically installed individually on servers or on systems with sensitive information. If users on any of these hosts try to perform any unauthorized operation, the host-based IDS will raise an alarm to the administrator. A host-based IDS is also useful in monitoring and detecting unauthorized file changes.

- **Log file monitoring**: This type of IDS searches through and analyzes log files of different network services to identify any traces of intrusion. For example, this type of IDS may search through a web server log file and check whether there have been any failed login attempts or any web attacks like XSS, SQL injection, and so on.

- **File integrity checking**: File integrity checkers monitor all sensitive files like configuration files for changes. They do so my keeping a record of the checksum values of all files at a given time. Any change in a file would change its checksum value and thus raise an alarm. If any Trojan or virus infects the system, many configuration files will be changed. Such intrusions and infections can be detected by file integrity checking. Tripwire offers applications for file integrity monitoring.

Evading an IDS

Most intrusion detection systems work on a signature basis. It's quite possible for the attacker to create a custom packet payload that won't match any of the signatures in the predefined database of the IDS. This way, the attacker can bypass the IDS and possibly compromise the remote system without creating any noisy alerts. Following are some of the techniques used to evade and bypass an IDS.

- **Insertion attack:** In an insertion attack, the attacker tries to confuse the IDS by sending invalid packets. The attacker crafts a malformed packet in such a way that the end system interprets the attack payload correctly but the IDS is unable to recognize the attack.

- **Denial of service:** Many IDS systems use a centralized logging server to log all events and alerts. If the attackers know the IP address of this centralized logging server, they can launch a denial-of-service attack on that server so that the IDS won't be able to log any more events.

- **Obfuscating and encoding:** Obfuscating means converting normal readable text or code into something that is hard to read and interpret. This is often used for security and privacy reasons. Encoding is a similar way of converting plain text into a special format and is mainly used for web transmissions. For example, if an attacker requests the URL http://example.com/php?id=<script>alert("XSS")</script> then the IDS might raise an alert since it has a Cross Site Scripting payload. However, an attacker might choose to encode it using BASE64 format and convert it to aHR0cDovL2V4YW1wbGUuY29tL3BocD9pZD08c2NyaXB0PmFsZXJ0KCJYU1MiKTwvc2N yaXB0Pg==. Now the IDS might treat this as normal text and forward it ahead without raising an alarm.

- **Session splicing and fragmentation:** *Session splicing* and *fragmentation* involve breaking, slicing, and splitting packets into multiple pieces such that no single packet causes the IDS to trigger an alert. Many IDS systems tend to ignore packet reconstruction before a packet is matched against the signature database.

- **Invalid packets**: Sending invalid TCP packets is another way of evading an IDS. An attacker can manipulate one of the six TCP flags or the packet checksum in order to pass it through the IDS.

- **Polymorphic shellcodes**: Most IDS systems have a standard default set of intrusion signatures. Attackers can modify the attack payload so that it doesn't match the default IDS signature and gets through it.

Common Symptoms of an Intrusion

Whenever there's an intrusion into a system (human or malware), it makes a lot of changes in various parts of the affected system. The intrusion might create new files or delete existing ones, change Registry entries, modify user accounts, and so on. Following are some of the signs of a possible intrusion:

- **Login failures for valid users**: In case of an intrusion or a compromise, the passwords of valid active users on the system may be changed or the accounts may be locked.

- **Active unused accounts**: Each system has some accounts that are rarely used. Such accounts include the system user accounts used for specific purposes. During or after an intrusion, such unused user accounts may appear to be active. Attackers often use such dormant accounts to get into the system.

- **Login during nonbusiness hours**: Every system maintains a record of the last login time for each user account. If there are couple of accounts whose last login is frequent during nonbusiness hours, it may be a sign of an intrusion.

- **Unusual system performance**: Let's assume an organization has a server which was running with 40% CPU consumption since last two months. Suddenly over a weekend the CPU consumption shoots to 95%. This might be a sign of intrusion. There's another server that is frequently crashing and rebooting since last couple of days. This again could be due to some kind of malicious intrusion.

- **Strange timestamps**: Every file and folder on the system has a timestamp associated with it, which includes the date and time when it was created, last modified, and accessed. If multiple files on the filesystem are showing strange and outdated timestamps, then it's a clear indication that some malicious program has tampered with the system.

- **Unknown processes and ports**: On a compromised system after a successful intrusion, there may be many unknown processes and ports open for connection with unknown remote hosts.

Firewalls

In simple layman terms, a *firewall* is computer hardware or software that helps protect systems from unauthorized access. The most basic function of a firewall is to set access control rules based on sockets. These firewall rules are designed according to the organization's security policy. For example, an organization might want to block access to the FTP server (Port 21) to all users outside its network while allowing all internal and external users access to the web server (Port 80). All such access requirements and policies can be translated into the form of firewall rules. The firewall monitors all inbound and outbound connections and allows or denies access according to these predefined rules.

DMZ

A *DMZ (demilitarized zone)* is a buffer area between a private intranet and the external public network. Any service that needs to be accessed from the external public network is placed in a DMZ. For example, a web server hosting a website is placed in a DMZ, but the database server associated with it is placed in the intranet.

Firewall Architecture

Correct placement of a firewall within the network is important in order to make the firewall work properly. If its placement within the network goes wrong, then even the latest and most sophisticated firewall will be of no use. Following are some of the architectural considerations for placement of firewalls.

- **Bastion host**: A *bastion host* is a special-purpose host computer that is placed outside the firewall or DMZ and is hardened to withstand external attacks. It generally hosts a single application. A bastion host is commonly used for hosting DNS, email, honeypots, proxy servers, VPNs, web servers, and so on.

- **Screened subnet**: A *screened subnet* is a type of network architecture that implements a single firewall with three network interfaces. One interface is used to connect to the external public network (Internet), another is used to connect to the DMZ, and the remaining is used to connect to the internal private network (intranet). This results in separation of the intranet from the DMZ and Internet.

- **Multi-homed firewall**: *Multi-homed architecture* involves two or more firewalls that connect separate network segments. Its specifications are designed according to the organization's security needs.

Types of Firewall

Based on their purpose and overall placement in the network, firewalls are of various types. Firewalls are also classified based on the OSI layer on which they operate. Following are a few types of commonly used firewalls:

- **Packet filters**: A *packet filter* firewall works at the Network layer of the OSI model and inspects every packet passing through to match against predefined access control lists. Following are some of the factors that the packet filter firewall uses to make decisions:

  - Source IP address

  - Destination IP address

  - Source port

  - Destination port

  - Direction: inbound / outbound

  - Network interface

- **Circuit-level gateways**: A *circuit-level gateway* firewall works at the Session layer of the OSI model. It doesn't filter individual packets. Instead, it monitors all requests for establishing new sessions and checks whether the TCP three-way handshake has been completed to verify the validity of a session.

- **Application-level gateways**: An application-level gateway firewall works at the Application layer of OSI model. This type of firewall filters traffic based on application-specific commands, such as HTTP GET or POST.

164

- **Stateful inspection firewalls**: A stateful inspection firewall combines features of packet filter firewalls, circuit-level gateways and application-level gateways. It intercepts and monitors all packets, filters them at the Network layer, verifies whether the established sessions are valid and authorized, and also evaluates contents of the packet at the Application layer.

Firewall Identification Techniques

A firewall is typically placed in a network to filter out unwanted traffic. The existence of a firewall is transparent to the end users. However, for security testing or penetration testing of a network, it is necessary to detect the presence of a firewall or any packet filtering device. If the place or position and type of firewall are known, then it can help craft custom attacks to bypass the firewall restrictions. Following are some of the ways used to identify the presence of a firewall in a network:

- **Port scanning**: *Port scanning* is one of the most common information-gathering techniques. It helps identify all open ports on the target system. It may be possible to detect a firewall running on a remote host if the firewall is running on its default port. For example, the Checkpoint firewall by default uses ports 256, 257, 258 and 259.

- **Firewalking**: *Firewalking* is a technique similar to tracerouting. It is used to scan and collect information about the remote hosts that are behind a firewall. It simply sends a TCP or UDP packet with a TTL value one hop greater than the targeted firewall. The response is analyzed to determine ACL filters and network map. It is a type of active reconnaissance.

Evading Firewalls

Firewalls are strategically placed in a network to filter out unwanted traffic and control the access to resources on the network. However, during a real-world attack or simulated penetration test, firewalls prove a major hurdle by blocking the attack traffic. Following are some of the ways of evading or bypassing the firewall restrictions:

- **IP address spoofing**: IP address spoofing is one of the effective ways of bypassing firewall restrictions. In this technique, the attacker changes the IP address of his host to that of a trusted host. To understand this, let's consider the following scenario:

  - There are four systems: A, B, C and D.

  - A is a server in the network, B is a firewall, C is one of the trusted hosts in the network, and D is the attacker.

  - Now if D tries to access A, it will be blocked by B.

  - To bypass this restriction, D changes its IP address to that of C, which is already trusted by B.

- **Source routing**: This technique allows the attacker to define the way or route the packet should take to reach its destination. This will help the attacker bypass the route where the firewall resides.

- **Bypassing the firewall using a proxy server**: Many organizations choose to block access to social websites from their intranet. Such restrictions can be bypassed using proxy servers. Since access to the proxy server isn't blocked, a user can connect to the proxy server, which can then connect to destination website on behalf of user. There are many such free proxy servers available openly on the Internet.

- **Tunneling (ICMP, HTTP)**: Because of stringent security policies, many organizations opt to open only limited ports on their firewall. For example, an organization may open up only port 80 and block all other ports. In such a scenario, an attacker can use tunneling techniques to pass other traffic through the port that is open. Tunneling encapsulates and wraps the traffic in the protocol format that is permitted through the firewall. For instance, all Telnet traffic can be wrapped in HTTP packet format so that it passes through port 80.

Honeypots

A *honeypot* is a system that is deliberately made vulnerable to attract and trap malicious attackers. It has no authorized users associated and doesn't have any business value. It is isolated in a way that only attackers can probe it with the intent of compromising the system. Once the attacker connects to the honeypot, the honeypot records all events and activities performed by the attacker. This helps the system administrator learn more about how the attacker compromised the system and then accordingly strengthen the security of other real systems within the network.

Figure 13-1 shows KFSensor, which is a Windows-based honeypot used to emulate different services.

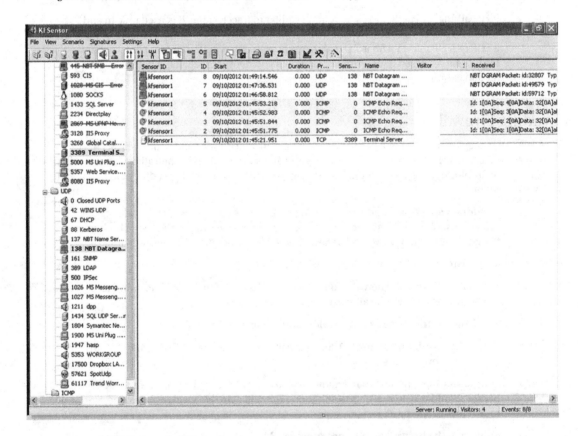

Figure 13-1. *Windows-based KFSensor honeypot for emulating various services*

Types of Honeypots

Honeypots are used to lure the attacker and divert her from attacking the real target. Based on how honeypots interact with the attacker, they can be classified as follows:

- **High-interaction honeypots**: This type of honeypot consists of a highly controlled network running various services. The attackers typically connect over encrypted SSH and try to break in further. All the activities of the attacker are recorded for further analysis. This is typically an isolated network with real applications and services. Hence, for an attacker it becomes very difficult to detect the presence of a honeypot.

- **Low-interaction honeypots**: This type of honeypot is typically an emulated service that has limited interactive capabilities. For example, while a connection over a real SSH would support all Linux commands, a connection over an emulated SSH will support only a limited set of commands. If any input beyond its predefined capability is given, it will throw an error making the attacker aware of the honeypot's presence.

Detecting Honeypots

We have seen that a honeypot is a system that is deliberately made vulnerable to attract attackers and divert them from attacking real systems. However, there are a few ways by which attackers could possibly detect the presence of a honeypot and target the real system instead:

- Attackers can detect a honeypot by probing and scanning all the services running on the system.

- Attackers can use tools like HPING to craft special packets, send them to the system, and determine the presence of a honeypot based on the responses.

- Attackers can use multiple proxy servers before connecting to the system (honeypot) so that their identity remains hidden.

- Attackers can also make use of tools like Send Safe Honeypot Hunter to automate the process of honeypot detection.

Summary

Following are the key takeaways from this chapter:

- An *IDS* is a system that monitors the network traffic and alerts the administrator when any type of intrusion is detected.

- *Insertion attacks, denial of service attacks, obfuscating/encoding, session splicing and fragmentation, sending invalid packets,* and *polymorphic shellcodes* are some of the techniques for evading and bypassing IDS.

- A *firewall* is computer hardware or software that helps protect systems from unauthorized access.

- A *bastion host* is a special-purpose host computer that is placed outside the firewall or DMZ and is hardened to withstand external attacks.

- A *screened subnet* is a type of network architecture that implements a single firewall with three network interfaces.

- *Multi-homed architecture* involves two or more firewalls that connect separate network segments.

- A *DMZ (demilitarized zone)* is a buffer area between a private intranet and the external public network.

- *Packet filter* firewalls work at the Network layer of the OSI model, *circuit-level gateways* work at the Session layer, and *application-level gateways* work at the Application layer of the OSI model.

- *IP address spoofing, source routing,* using *proxy servers* and *tunneling* are some of the techniques for evading and bypassing firewalls.

- A *honeypot* is a system that is deliberately made vulnerable to attract and trap malicious attackers.

Do-It-Yourself Exercises

1. Download, install and explore the KFSensor honeypot.

2. Explore various ways of crafting IP packets with the HPING tool.

Sample Questions: Test Your Knowledge

1. A bastion host is a special-purpose host computer which is placed inside the firewall or DMZ and is hardened to withstand external attacks. True or false?

   a. True

   b. False

2. At which layer of the OSI model does the circuit-level gateway firewall work?

   a. Layer 2

   b. Layer 1

   c. Layer 5

   d. Layer 7

3. Which of the following architectures involves two or more firewalls that connect separate network segments?

   a. Screened subnet

   b. Multi-homed firewall

   c. Gateway firewall

   d. None of the above

4. A honeypot running emulated services with limited capability is known as?

   a. Medium-interaction honeypot

   b. High-interaction honeypot

   c. Low-interaction honeypot

   d. None of the above

5. Which of the following techniques involves encapsulating data in some other protocol format?

   a. Source routing

   b. Tunneling

   c. Proxy server

   d. IP spoofing

CHAPTER 14

Cryptography

There has always been a need to keep data confidential while at rest and while in transit. So far, there have been various ways and techniques used for keeping data confidential; however, these techniques have become more complex and robust with advancements in computing technology. This chapter introduces key concepts in cryptography along with its practical applications.

Key Topics Cryptography, symmetric vs asymmetric encryption, types of ciphers, cryptography tools, message digest, secure shell, PKI, SSL certificates, digital signatures, SSL and TLS.

Cryptography and Its Objectives

Let's break the word *cryptography* into its parts, *crypto* and *graphy*. In the dictionary meaning, *crypto* means something that is concealed and secret, and *graphy* means a descriptive science. Thus cryptography is the science of converting normal plain-text data into some other format that is readable only by authorized persons. In our daily life we do many transactions, like send emails, chat on messengers, perform financial transactions, and much more. All of these activities involve private data that if disclosed to an unauthorized person could lead to severe damage. Cryptography plays a major role in protecting such private, sensitive, and confidential data. In very simple terms, cryptography is a process of converting plain text into cipher text. It is important to note that cryptography has been in use since historic times and has only changed its form to suit modern-day needs. Cryptography aims to provide the following:

- Confidentiality
- Integrity
- Authentication
- Nonrepudiation

Types of Cryptography

Cryptography involves the use of an algorithm and a key. The key is usually preshared between the parties involved in the communication. Based on the type of key being used for encryption and decryption, there are two types of encryption.

© Sagar Ajay Rahalkar 2016

S.A. Rahalkar, *Certified Ethical Hacker (CEH) Foundation Guide*, DOI 10.1007/978-1-4842-2325-3_14

Symmetric Encryption

In *symmetric key encryption* the same key is used for both encryption and decryption. The parties involved in this must have access to the encryption key. It works faster than asymmetric encryption and is simple to implement. However, the major risk is the encryption key being leaked or compromised. If the encryption key is stolen by any means, then any person possessing that key will be able to encrypt and decrypt data in an unauthorized manner.

Asymmetric Encryption

Asymmetric encryption overcomes the security concern with using symmetric encryption. Asymmetric encryption uses separate keys for encryption and decryption. The key used for encrypting the data is referred to as the *public key*, while the key used for decrypting the data is referred to as the *private key*. Although this makes the process a bit more complex and slower than symmetric encryption, it certainly offers better protection against the risk of keys being compromised. Asymmetric encryption is also known as *public-key cryptography*. To understand how asymmetric encryption works, consider the following example, in which A wants to send some confidential data to B using asymmetric encryption:

1. A will use B's public key to encrypt the data to be sent.

2. A will send the encrypted data to B.

3. B will use his own private key to decrypt the data sent by A.

■ **Note**   It is not possible to derive the private key by knowing the public key or vice-versa. The private key and public key are different entities, and each of them is used for a different purpose.

Key Escrow

In the context of the rise in terrorist activities around the world, encrypted data has become a major hurdle to government investigating agencies. Modern-day cipher algorithms are so strong that data once encrypted cannot be decrypted without having the right key. Thus the concept of *key escrow* has come into existence, which enables government agencies to store copies of keys that can be used for decrypting data without the knowledge of the owner. With all the regulations in place, key escrow allows only limited authorized individuals within government agencies to use the keys in investigating cases mainly of national importance.

Types of Ciphers

A *cipher* is a method, formula, or algorithm for writing information in a secret or disguised manner. On a high level, ciphers can be classified as follows; a comparison is provided in Table 14-1:

- **Classical Ciphers**: Classical ciphers are a very basic type of cipher that performs simple operations on alphabets. They can be implemented manually or using mechanical devices. However, they are not very reliable for commercial use. Classical ciphers can be further classified into two types:

- **Substitution cipher**: This is a simple cipher that replaces bits, characters, or blocks of characters with different bits, characters, or blocks.

- **Transposition cipher**: In this type of cipher, letters from plain text are shifted so that the cipher text contains a permutation of the plain text.

Modern ciphers: Compared to the classical ciphers, modern ciphers use stronger and more complex mathematical algorithms and formulas to transform plain text into cipher text. This ensures that the cipher text is protected against common cryptography attacks. Modern day ciphers can be further classified as follows:

Based on the type of key used:

- **Private key cryptography**: This is referred to as symmetric key encryption, where the same key is used for encrypting as well as decrypting the data.

- **Public key cryptography**: This is referred to as asymmetric key encryption. where different keys are used for encrypting and decrypting the data.

Based on the type of input data:

- **Block ciphers**: In this method, a cryptographic algorithm is applied to a block of data rather than one bit at a time.

- **Stream ciphers**: In this method, a cryptographic algorithm is applied to one character at a time to produce the output cipher text.

Table 14-1. *Cipher Comparison: Differences between Various Encryption Algorithms with Key Strengths*

Factor	DES	AES	RSA
Full Name	Data Encryption Standard	Advanced Encryption Standard	Named after the founders Rivest, Shamir and Adleman
Developed in Year	1977	2000	1978
Key Length	138, 192, 256 Bits	128, 192, 256 Bits	More than 1024 Bits
Type of Algorithm	Symmetric	Symmetric	Asymmetric
Algorithm Speed	Fast	Fast	Fast

Factor	RC4	RC5	RC6
Full Name			
Developed in Year	1987	1994	1998
Type of Algorithm	Stream Cipher	Block Cipher	Block Cipher
Key Size in Bits	40 and 64	128	0-2040; commonly 128, 192 or 256

Cryptography Tools

The classical ciphers were based on a simple formula, and they can be implemented by manual calculations as well. Modern ciphers, however, involve complex algorithms that cannot be computed manually. There are many tools available that ease the process of encryption and decryption. One such tool is Advanced Encryption Package, which allows us to encrypt and decrypt files using multiple algorithms (Figure 14-1).

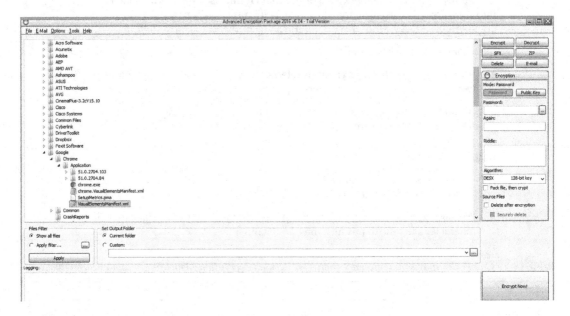

Figure 14-1. *Advanced Encryption Package tool for encrypting files*

The left pane allows you to select the file to encrypt, and the right pane provides options for selecting the key and type of encryption algorithm.

Message Digests

Cryptography is essentially used for converting plain text into cipher text to ensure confidentiality. If a user has the appropriate key, the cipher text can be reversed to get the original plain text. A *message digest* or *hash* is a technique used to verify and assure the integrity of data. Unlike encryption, a message digest is a one-way function. This means you cannot recover the original data from the hashed data. Using a particular algorithm, if we calculate the message digest of a string, then the message digest will remain unchanged as long as the string remains unchanged. Even the least change, like adding a space or punctuation mark will completely change its corresponding message digest value. The message digest algorithm transforms input of any length into output of fixed length.

As an example, consider Table 14-2, which has two strings with their corresponding message digest values calculated using the MD5 algorithm.

Table 14-2. *Difference in Hash Values of Two Strings with Minor Difference*

String	MD5 checksum value
Hello World	B10A8DB164E0754105B7A99BE72E3FE5
Hello World!	ED076287532E86365E841E92BFC50D8C

We can see in this example that just by adding a single exclamation mark, the message digest value completely changed. This shows that each piece of data has a unique message digest value, just as we human beings have unique fingerprints.

Table 14-3 shows some commonly used message digest algorithms along with their respective output strength in bits.

Table 14-3. *Hashing Algorithms with Output Size in Bits*

Algorithm	Output size in Bits
MD2	128
MD4	128
MD5	128
RIPEMD	128
RIPEMD-160	160
RIPEMD-320	320
SHA-0	160
SHA-1	160
SHA-224, SHA-256	224/256
SHA3-384	384
SHA3-512	512
WHIRLPOOL	512

Message digests are widely used in cryptography, digital signatures, and for validating the authenticity of digital evidence.

There are many free tools and websites available that help you calculate the message digest of a file or a string. One such website is http://onlinemd5.com/.

In Figure 14-2 we uploaded a file named Sample.txt and selected the algorithm type as MD5. The website instantly calculated the message digest (referred to as the checksum).

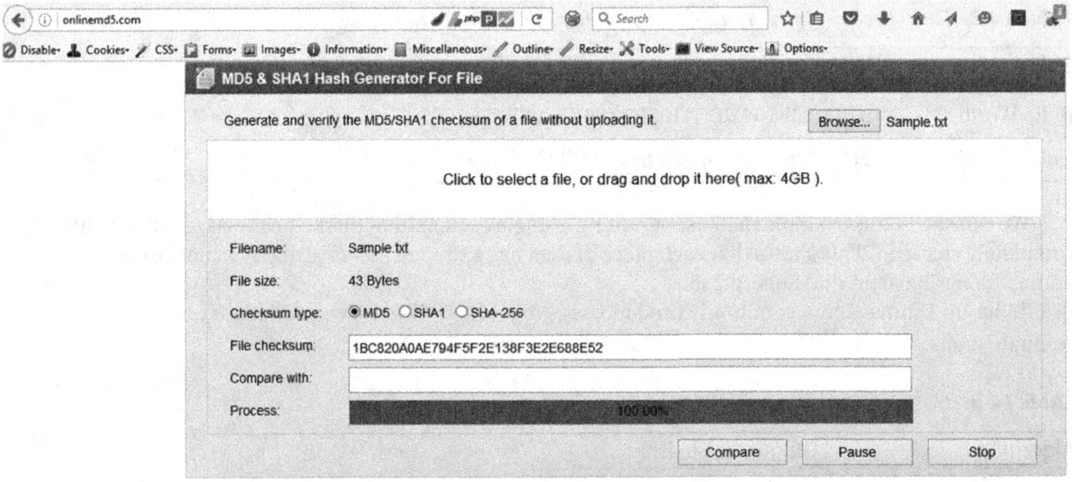

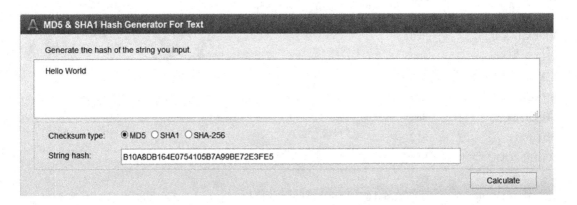

Figure 14-2. *Free online tool for calculating message digest of any given file*

We can also use the same website for generating the message digest of a string, as shown in Figure 14-3.

Figure 14-3. *Calculating the hash value of a string using various hashing algorithms*

Secure Shell (SSH)

Secure shell is a program that helps connect to a system over the network in a secure way. Once connected, users can work on the remote system as if they have physical access to it. It is often used as a replacement for Telnet, which is less secure, since it doesn't encrypt the data during the session. SSH is commonly used for the following:

- Secure file transfer over an untrusted network

- Remote administration and command execution

- Securing applications by passing their traffic through SSH (using port forwarding)

SSH uses TCP port 22 for all its connections.

PKI

Public key infrastructure (PKI) is collectively a set of mechanisms, procedures, and policies that form a framework for addressing fundamental aspects of security like confidentiality, integrity, nonrepudiation, authentication, and access control. PKI essentially helps in establishing the trust relationship between different entities of the digital world.

Common PKI Terminology

The public key infrastructure is essentially a framework for providing various aspects of security (like confidentiality, integrity, authentication, and so on) and involves many components and entities that work together. Following are some of the key entities that are involved in the functioning of PKI.

- **Certifying authority**: The certifying or certificate authority (CA) is the entity responsible for issuing the digital certificates. It binds the requestor's identity to the corresponding public key.

- **Registration authority**: A registration authority verifies a user request for a digital certificate and tells the CA to issue it.

- **Digital certificate**: Digital certificates are similar to ID cards in the real world. Digital certificates helps verify identities of individuals, organizations, and computers.

- **Digital signature**: A digital signature is equivalent to the physical signature and is used to sign digital documents. It helps prove the identity and authenticity of the document.

- **Certificate revocation lists (CRL)**: A CRL is a list of all the certificates that have been revoked. Hence if a certificate is listed in the CRL, it no longer should be trusted.

Components and Types of an SSL Certificate

Based on the type of application, there are two common types of certificates, known as *self-signed certificates* (Figure 14-4) and *CA-signed certificates*. A self-signed certificate is generated and signed by the same identity whose identity it certifies. This type of certificate is free of cost and can be generated quickly using tools like OpenSSL. However, self-signed certificates are mainly used for internal or testing purpose and cannot be trusted for professional or commercial use.

A CA-signed certificate is issued by an authorized certifying authority. The CA does all the verification and validation before granting the certificate. Hence for commercial applications, CA signed certificates are used and trusted. Entrust, Verizon, and Symantec are some of the commonly used certifying authorities.

Just because a website has installed an SSL certificate, doesn't mean it's completely secure. The certificate has several components that must be validated before trusting it.

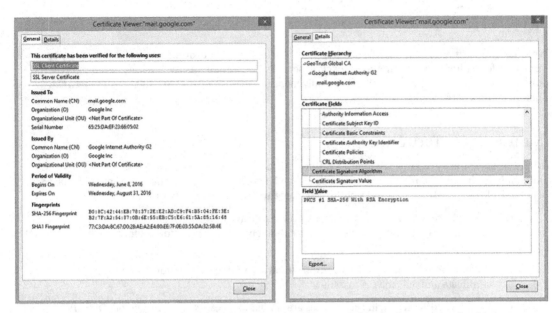

Figure 14-4. *SSL certificate details including its issuing authority, validity, and encryption/hashing algorithms used*

Upon viewing the SSL certificate, you can obtain information like who has issued the certificate, its serial number, the domain for which it is valid, and—most important—details about its expiry. An expired SSL certificate is equivalent to having no certificate at all.

Testing an SSL Certificate

There are a couple of free standalone as well as online tools that help test the strength or weakness of a given SSL certificate. One such online utility is available at https://www.ssllabs.com/ssltest/. Simply surf to this URL and enter the domain name whose certificate you want to test (Figure 14-5).

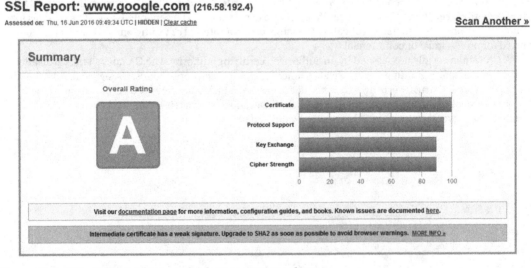

Figure 14-5. *SSL certificate test report for domain www.google.com*

The tool gives a detailed analysis report about the strengths and weaknesses of the SSL certificate being tested.

Digital Signatures

A digital signature is the digital equivalent of a physical signature, which helps to prove the authenticity of the digital message or document. By verifying the digital signature, the recipient can trust that the message was created and sent by a known sender, and the sender also cannot deny sending the message. In this way, the interests of both parties, sender and receiver, are secured. To understand how a digital signature works, let's consider following example. A wants to send the message "Hello" to B, along with a digital signature. This involves the following steps, carried out by each party's email software:

1. A will first calculate the message digest (hash) of the message to be sent (in this case "Hello").

2. Once the hash of the message to be sent is generated, A will encrypt the hash with his own private key. The resulting output is known as a digital signature.

3. A will now append the generated digital signature to the message and send it to B.

4. B will receive the message from A along with the digital signature.

5. B will now decrypt the digital signature using A's public key and extract the hash.

6. B will then compute the hash of the message received (in this case "Hello").

7. If the hash calculated by B and the hash extracted from A's digital signature match exactly, then B can trust the message and confirm it has been sent by A only. If in any way the two hashes don't match, that implies either there has been some tampering of the message while in transit or the message has been sent by some forged individual other than A.

SSL and TLS

SSL stands for secure socket layer and is a popular type of public-key cryptography. It was developed by Netscape and is widely used by browsers and web servers to transmit user data securely. The following example explains in brief how SSL works:

1. The user's browser makes a request to secure socket (commonly port 443).

2. The remote server responds with its SSL certificate.

3. The user's browser encrypts the session key with the server's public key and sends it to the server.

4. The server verifies the key and indicates that all future transmissions will be encrypted.

5. The browser and server can now communicate securely over an encrypted channel.

TLS stands for transport layer security and is the successor to SSL. Like SSL, TLS also provides secure communication on Internet. There are minor differences between SSL 3.0 and TLS 1.0; however, the base protocol remains almost the same.

Data That Can Be Encrypted

Right from a single bit to a complete hard-drive, everything can be encrypted. But the question is whether the data is worth encrypting. The process of encryption consumes CPU and memory resources, so it can be an overhead if data is encrypted unnecessarily. Hence it is important to identify data that is sensitive and needs to be protected from unauthorized access. Only such data should be chosen for encryption. There are two primary principles for encryption:

- **Encryption of data at rest/storage**: This principle states that all the sensitive data that is at rest—that is, stored in any form of memory (hard drive, flash drive, or whatever)—should be encrypted.

- **Encryption of data in transit**: This principle requires that all the sensitive data that is traveling using some form of communication should be encrypted. For example, the username and password should be encrypted while logging into a website. This is commonly achieved using HTTPS.

Commonly encryption is applied to the following entities:

- **Fields of a database**: Applications often store sensitive user information like passwords, PINs, payment information, and so on in databases. All such database fields storing sensitive private information are encrypted. In many countries, this is a legal requirement to ensure the privacy of the users.

- **Files**: Single files containing sensitive information are encrypted to keep data confidential.

- **Email**: Because the email travels over the untrusted public network, there's always a risk of interception and eavesdropping. Hence email messages are quite often encrypted to keep the data confidential.

- **Drive or whole disk**: A single drive or whole disk can be encrypted based on the sensitivity of data it contains. Windows has a utility called BitLocker, which helps encrypt an entire hard drive. Another application, TrueCrypt, helps create virtual encrypted containers, which can be mounted as drives.

Attacks on Cryptography and Cryptanalysis

Cryptanalysis is the process of attacking or breaking the cryptographic algorithm without knowledge of the key. Most modern algorithms are strong and resilient enough to withstand such attacks. However some algorithms do have vulnerabilities that could be exploited to break the cipher.

- **Cipher text-only attack**: This is a basic type of attack where the attacker sniffs the traffic to get cipher text. The attacker will have access to the cipher text of several messages, all of which are encrypted using same algorithm.

- **Adaptive chosen plain text attack**: In this type of attack the attacker chooses input to the encryption algorithm based on prior results.

- **Known plain text attack**: In this type of attack the attacker has access to both plain text and cipher text and uses this information to reveal further secret information like keys and codes.

- **Rubber horse attack**: In this type the attacker threatens or blackmails the victim unless he hands over the encryption keys.

Summary

Following are this chapter's key points and concepts:

- *Cryptography* is the science of converting plain-text data into some other format that is readable only by authorized persons.

- *Symmetric encryption* uses the same key for encryption and decryption, while *asymmetric encryption* uses different keys for encryption and decryption.

- *Key escrow* allows only limited authorized individuals within government agencies to use the keys in investigating cases mainly of national importance.

- A *message digest* or *hash* is used to verify the integrity of data and unlike encryption, it is irreversible.

- *Cryptanalysis* is the process of attacking or breaking the cryptographic algorithm without knowledge of the key.

Do-It-Yourself (DIY) Exercises

1. Create a simple text file and type some text in it. Save it and calculate its hash value using the MD5 algorithm. Now reopen the text file, change some text, and save it. Now again calculate the hash value of the text file using the MD5 algorithm. Compare the two hash values.

2. Go to `https://www.ssllabs.com/ssltest/` and test the SSL certificate of any website of your choice.

3. Download, install, and explore various encryption options in the tool Advanced Encryption Package (`www.aeppro.com/`).

Test Your Knowledge: Sample Questions

1. Cryptography provides which of the following features?

    a. Confidentiality

    b. Integrity

    c. Availability

    d. All of the above

2. A public key and private key pair is used in symmetric encryption. True or False?

    a. True

    b. False

3. A transposition cipher is a simple cipher that replaces bits, characters, or blocks of characters with different bits, characters, or blocks. True or False?

    a. True

    b. False

4. Which of the following is a program that helps connect to a system over the network in a secure way?

    a. SSL

    b. TLS

    c. Both a and b

    d. Only a

5. Enterprise applications prefer to use which of the following certificates?

    a. Self-signed

    b. CA-signed

    c. Root-signed

    d. None of the above

6. The message digest of a text is reversible. True or False?

    a. True

    b. False

■ ■ ■

Career Tracks Available after CEH

The goal of this appendix is to introduce the various certifications related to Information Security and provide tips on building a successful career in Information Security.

According to a recent report from *Forbes*, the cyber security market is expected to grow from $75 Billion in 2015 to $170 Billion by 2020. According to another survey, there are around 209,000 vacant cyber security jobs in the United States. This clearly indicates that there is a huge demand for cyber security professionals worldwide. The leaders of major economies are also expressing serious concerns over the cyber security threats to their nations. With this being said, this appendix introduces some of the most in-demand Information Security certifications and some add-on tips to take your professional career to next level.

Certifications

There are literally dozens of certifications available on the market. This section lists some of the best and most in-demand certifications from various domains of Information Security.

The Network Security Track

This track helps you learn how to install, configure, deploy and manage various network security devices, like firewalls, intrusion detection systems, intrusion prevention systems, VPNs, and so on. Cisco offers certifications for gaining in-depth knowledge in network security systems. Following are a few of the certifications related to network security:

Certification	Description	Vendor
CCNA	Cisco Certified Network Associate	Cisco
CCNA Security	Cisco Certified Network Associate with specialization in Security	Cisco
CCNP Security	Cisco Certified Network Professional with specialization in Security	Cisco
CCIE Security	Cisco Certified Internetworking Expert with specialization in Security	Cisco
ArcSight ESM Security Administrator and Analyst	SIEM Certification	HP
Splunk Administrator or Splunk Certified Architect	Log Management	Splunk

© Sagar Ajay Rahalkar 2016
S.A. Rahalkar, *Certified Ethical Hacker (CEH) Foundation Guide*, DOI 10.1007/978-1-4842-2325-3

The Forensics Track

This track involves getting hands-on knowledge and skills related to computer forensics. Professionals with computer forensic skills are required in both the private and public sectors for investigating various frauds and cybercrime incidents.

Certification	Description	Vendor
CHFI	Certified Hacking Forensic Investigator	EC-Council
ECE	EnCASE Certified Examiner	Guidance Software
ADCE	Access Data Certified Examiner	Access Data
FOR508	Advanced Digital Forensics and Incident Response	SANS
FOR610	Reverse Engineering Malware – Malware Analysis Tools and Techniques	SANS
CCFP	Certified Cyber Forensics Professional	ISC2

The Auditing Track

This includes certifications that aim at providing insights on auditing information systems based on various standards.

Certification	Description	Vendor
ISO 27001 LA	ISO 27001 Lead Auditor	IRCA
CISA	Certified Information Systems Auditor	ISACA

The Security Testing Track

The security testing track includes certifications that teach about performing vulnerability assessments, penetration testing, and the like.

Certification	Description	Vendor
CEH	Certified Ethical Hacker	EC-Council
ECSA/LPT	EC-Council Certified Security Analyst / Licensed Penetration Tester	EC-Council
OSCP	Offensive Security Certified Professional	Offensive Security
OSCE	Offensive Security Certified Expert	Offensive Security
GPEN	GIAC Penetration Tester	Global Information Assurance Certification (GIAC)

The Information Security General Track

Following are a few of the certifications that cover managerial aspect of Information Security. This includes learning governance, risk management, and related topics.

Certification	Description	Vendor
CISSP	Certified Information Systems Security Professional	ISC2
CISM	Certified Information Security Manager	ISACA
CRISC	Certified in Risk and Information Systems Control	ISACA
CCSK	Certificate of Cloud Security Knowledge	Cloud Security Alliance

The Next Steps

In this appendix, we have seen a wide list of Information Security certifications that you could opt for depending on your specific areas of interest. However, in addition to from these certifications, there are a couple of things that need to be done in order to strengthen your skills and then build your career.

Learning Programming Languages

In the field of Information Security, it is essential to know at least few of the common programming languages. That gives you the power to automate things and perform tasks more efficiently. A few of the programming languages worth learning are:

- C
- PHP
- Python
- Java Script
- SQL Basics
- Macros using VB
- Basics of Assembly Language
- Shell Scripting
- PowerShell

The following sections feature tips on how to improve your profile.

Bug Bounty

Bug Bounty is a program where organizations acknowledge or pay remuneration to whoever finds security issues in their applications. Finding a security bug in a website or mobile app and reporting it to the concerned organization gives you a great amount of confidence. It also readily demonstrates your skills to prospective employers.

See https://bugcrowd.com/list-of-bug-bounty-programs for a list of bug bounty programs announced by various organizations across the globe.

Social Presence

Social networking platforms can be effectively used to network with the community and increase visibility. LinkedIn can be used to build a profile snapshot and connect with other professional peers. Facebook can be used to create a page or community and share your thoughts on topics of interest.

Speaking at Information Security Conferences

There are many Information Security events and conferences across the globe around the year. Participating in such conferences to present on any of the research work you may have done is significantly beneficial. Your voice will be heard by a network of likeminded professionals. These are some of the top Information Security Conferences around the world:

Conference	Website
ShmooCon	https://shmoocon.org/
RSA Conference	http://www.rsaconference.com/
HITBSecConf	http://conference.hitb.org/
DerbyCon	https://www.derbycon.com/
DEF CON	https://www.defcon.org/index.html
Black Hat	http://blackhat.com/
AppSec Europe	http://2016.appsec.eu/
ToorCon	https://toorcon.net/
NULLCON	http://nullcon.net
RUXCON	https://ruxcon.org.au/

Publishing Articles and Research Papers in Magazines

Many local and international magazines and journals publish articles on various topics of Information Security. There's a distinguished advantage in presenting and publishing articles in such media. Your work reaches a larger audience across the world. A few such magazines are:

- *Pentest Magazine*
- *Hackin9*
- *Hackinsight*
- *SC Magazine*

Developing Tools

There are many tools already for automating various security related tasks. However, there might be many problem areas for which there are no tools yet. Such areas should be identified, studied, and researched. A tool could be developed to solve a particular problem related to Information Security. Modern programming languages like Python make it easy for anyone to develop custom tools. Once the tool is developed, it can be shared through public communities like GitHub. Contributing something new to the community adds substantial value to your profile.

APPENDIX B

■ ■ ■

Interview Questions

This appendix presents various questions you're likely to be asked by prospective employers when you interview for a job position after completion of CEH. These questions tend to test the overall security aptitude as well as technical competence of the candidate.

- What is the difference between encoding, encryption and hashing?
- What is the difference between proxy, firewall, IDS, and IPS?
- How does asymmetric encryption work?
- How does SSL work?
- What is TLS and how is it different from SSL?
- Can you name a critical vulnerability found in SSL during recent times?
- What is port scanning? How can port scanning be prevented?
- What is a man-in-the-middle attack? Can it be prevented?
- What is the difference between false positive and false negative?
- What does the term "defense in depth" mean?
- What is a stateful inspection by a firewall?
- What is a DMZ? Which systems should be placed in DMZ?
- Is SSH completely secure?
- What is BYOD and what are the common security concerns associated with it?
- What are the different layers of the OSI model? Explain each layer in brief.
- What are honeypots?
- How do you keep yourself updated with the latest trends in Information Security?
- Which OS do you feel is more secure, Linux or Windows?
- How does Kerberos work?
- What is a zero-day vulnerability? Can it be prevented?
- What is a rainbow table attack? How can it be prevented?
- What is the difference between hub, switch, and router?

© Sagar Ajay Rahalkar 2016
S.A. Rahalkar, *Certified Ethical Hacker (CEH) Foundation Guide*, DOI 10.1007/978-1-4842-2325-3

- What are some common security concerns in Cloud computing?

- What is the difference between vulnerability assessment and penetration testing?

- What are the high-level steps to perform vulnerability assessment and penetration testing?

- What tools do you normally use for vulnerability assessment and penetration testing? Which tool you find the best and why?

- Is it possible to hack into a system without using any tool?

- What is the difference between active and passive information gathering?

- How does HTTPS make a website secure?

- What is a SQL injection attack? What are its types?

- What is a XSS attack? What are its types?

- What is CSRF? How can you prevent it?

- What is the difference between white box application security testing and black box application security testing?

- What standards do you refer to for web application security and related vulnerabilities?

- Will a Layer 3 firewall be useful in protecting the web application against common attacks? If yes, then to what extent?

- How does HTTP handle state?

- How do you identify that an application is vulnerable to blind SQL injection attack?

- What are the top five mobile application security threats?

- What is the difference between a standard, a policy, and a procedure?

- Name a vulnerability for each OSI layer.

■ ■ ■

Answers for Sample Questions

Chapter 1- Operating Systems

1. a
2. c
3. d
4. a
5. b
6. b
7. c
8. b

Chapter 2 - Database basics

1. c
2. b
3. d
4. b
5. d
6. d
7. b
8. c
9. c
10. a

© Sagar Ajay Rahalkar 2016
S.A. Rahalkar, *Certified Ethical Hacker (CEH) Foundation Guide*, DOI 10.1007/978-1-4842-2325-3

Chapter 3 - Networking Basics

1. a
2. b
3. b
4. c
5. c
6. d
7. b
8. d
9. b
10. c

Chapter 4- Programming Basics

1. b
2. c
3. b
4. d
5. d
6. d
7. c
8. a

Chapter 5- Virtualization and cloud basics

1. c
2. b
3. a
4. d
5. c

Chapter 6- Information Security Basics

1. b
2. c
3. b
4. c
5. b
6. c
7. d

Chapter 7 - Penetration Testing

1. d
2. c
3. a
4. c
5. c
6. a
7. b

Chapter 8 - Information Gathering

1. b
2. c
3. b
4. c
5. c

Chapter 9 - Hacking Basics

1. d
2. a
3. c
4. d

Chapter 10 - Web Application Hacking

1. b
2. b
3. c
4. c

Chapter 11 - Wireless Hacking

1. b
2. b
3. b

Chapter 12 - Mobile hacking

1. b
2. a
3. c
4. c
5. c

Chapter 13 - IDS and Honeypots

1. b
2. c
3. b
4. c
5. b

Chapter 14 - Cryptography

1. d
2. b
3. a
4. c
5. b
6. b

Index

Get the eBook for only $4.99!

Why limit yourself?

Now you can take the weightless companion with you wherever you go and access your content on your PC, phone, tablet, or reader.

Since you've purchased this print book, we are happy to offer you the eBook for just $4.99.

Convenient and fully searchable, the PDF version enables you to easily find and copy code—or perform examples by quickly toggling between instructions and applications.

To learn more, go to http://www.apress.com/us/shop/companion or contact support@apress.com.